END OVERWHELM NOW!

A Proven Process For Regaining Control Over Your Life

May this book help you End Overwhelm now! Wishing you all the best.

Karen

Kare[n]

End Overwhelm Now

Copyright © 2017 by Live Well Coaching and Karen Van Cleve.

ISBN 978-0-9786461-9-6 (paperback)
1.   Business & Money – Women & Business
2.   Self-Help – Emotions

www.EndOverwhelmNow.com
www.facebook.com/endoverwhelmnow
www.pinterest.com/coachkaren0217
www.LinkedIn/in/KarenVanCleve

Van Cleve, Karen, 1956 –
    End Overwhelm Now: A Proven Process For Regaining Control Over Your Life / Karen Van Cleve. – 1st ed.

Printed in the United States of America. For information, address Live Well Coaching, P.O. Box 150631, Lakewood, Colorado 80215.

Cover and interior design by Maryann Brown Sperry

For bulk orders, please contact Karen Van Cleve at Karen@EndOverwhelmNow.com

Acknowledgements

*"At times, our own light goes out and is rekindled by a spark
from another person. Each of us has cause to think with deep
gratitude of those who have lighted the flame within us."*
~ Albert Schweitzer

There are so many people who contributed both directly and indirectly to this book.

I first want to acknowledge my clients who taught me about the challenges of overwhelm, and who also taught me that there is a solution. I am inspired daily by the power and resilience of the human spirit and our infinite capacity for change.

I also want to acknowledge Tony Robbins for being a role model, a teacher, and an inspiration. I am forever grateful for the impact that you have had on my life. I am committed to using that to pay it forward and be a force for good in my way.

Thank you to my fellow coaches at Robbins Research. What an environment to be both loved and challenged to step up. You inspire me to keep being a better version of myself.

It took a village of advisors, contributors and reviewers to bring this project to fruition. First, my forever gratitude to my amazing editor, Maury Cohen of Editrix. She challenged me and helped to bring this book to a whole new level.

I am deeply grateful to my book coach, Orvel Ray Wilson. You taught me how to distill my thinking into coherent text. Quite a feat. And I am also grateful to my ghost writer, Howard Rankin. You helped shake my thinking loose to create the STORIES process that is at the heart of this book.

It takes a special friend to stand by you through the ups and downs of writing a book, and to actually read that book all the way through, even multiple times. A special thanks to the consistent encouragement of Terri Norvell, Mary Ellen Merrigan, Amy Terry, and Gail Fraser. Your support through the long journey will be special to me always. I'm grateful for the reviewers who contributed their feedback, insights and support: Brian Smiley, Chris Anderson, Donna DeMaria, Jayni Breaux, Jennifer Chalk, Meggan Auld, Nick Piercy, Sally Carruthers, and Shelley Sims.

To my coach, Carol Swanson, and my coaching buddy, Sara Basloe, thank you for your unwavering belief and accountability. And to my various mastermind partners who make a difference in my life: Rachelle Disbennett-Lee, John Marx, Laurie Taylor, Tom Dearth, Carl Swanson, Janet Pike, Marcia Cope and Marilyn Hajick. Thank you.

And finally, none of this would have happened without the unfailing support of my husband, Joel. Through the starts and stops, the times when I stumbled out of my office brain-dead, cranky, or both, he encouraged me. And for the last year, about every two weeks, he asked, "Is your book finished yet?" Well, Babe, you finally have your answer!

Contents

Introduction

You're overwhelmed.

This feeling may be a new experience, happening in response to changing life- conditions, or it may be something you've lived with for a long time. Either way, you need a way out.

I get it.

End Overwhelm Now is the book I needed during a time that I was in constant overwhelm and couldn't see any way out. The good news is, there is a solution to your overwhelm; and I can absolutely help you end your struggle. More good news is that the key is already within you, but more about that later.

When you're overwhelmed, it feels like you're dealing with more than any human can handle -- and you often are. That's why your To Do list can trigger such a powerful overwhelm response. You're running a race you can't possibly win. The result is frantic thoughts and feelings about how you're going to manage it all.

Overwhelm actually has a biological basis. Our ancestors had to keep up with everything in their environments . . . or die. Cave life was hard. There was a lot to do, with all that hunting, gathering and mating. In addition to the tools to make, hides to tan and pictures to draw on walls, there was a lot to worry about: dangerous weather, saber tooth tigers, eating the wrong berry. Even today, in many areas of the world, those who don't manage all the dangers around them won't survive to pass along their genes. This survival instinct has been honed over thousands of years of evolution.

We've inherited the instinct, but we live in a world where we can't possibly keep up with everything going on around us. Our culture amplifies the notion of "getting it all done" as the new drive to survive, but it's just not possible. Our ancestors only had to navigate a range of a few miles while we have world crises and events bombarding us 24/7, as well as mankind's collective knowledge of the universe available anywhere at any time on our radar screens through the smart phones we can't live without. We're saturated with constant communications through voice mail and email and text messages and Facebook and Twitter accounts which we are constantly tracking. Our lives are complicated with work and kids and houses and cars and computers and family and medical concerns and fitness and eating right and electronics and security. We live in a time with unprecedented rates of change, and are presented with more tasks and more choices than we can possibly manage. It's a losing battle.

But Wait! There's Hope

Although our world may seem by its very nature to throw us into overwhelm, there's a secret to making it all manageable. And when I tell you what it is, you will probably consider putting down this book to seek some other resource.

But I'm asking you trust me.

Because I know *exactly* what I'm talking about.

I have been studying overwhelm for most of the 15 years I've been coaching. I cured myself of feeling constantly overwhelmed and have successfully coached thousands of clients to do the same.
But still, when I tell you the basis of my system, you will doubt very much that I know what I'm talking about.

That's okay.

I get it.

Because what I am going to tell you is that the answer to your problem of overwhelm lies within you.

The tools I'm going to offer are tools for creating *internal* shifts in your life, not changing what's going on on the outside.

You probably picked up this book hoping I could teach you some systems or tricks for better managing your life so you won't be so overwhelmed.

And I will.

But not in the way you think.

Because no matter how it appears, **overwhelm doesn't come from what's going on "out there"** ... no matter how much you're juggling. It doesn't come from finding a way to do more, nor does it come from finding a way to do less. The answer doesn't lie "out there" at all.

What I have learned is that what's outside of us is actually a *trigger* for overwhelm; it's not the cause. And if the cause isn't "out there" the solution can't be either.

This book will wake you from the trance created by our crazy, chaotic world and restore you to sanity. But maybe not in the way you thought or expected.

The purpose of this book is to show you how to take charge of your life in a new way. It will cure you of feeling constantly overwhelmed by starting with the premise that you will end your struggle with feeling overwhelmed on a daily basis by making a shift on the **inside**.

You seldom can change the world "out there," but you absolutely have the power to change your thinking and behaviors.

This will, in turn, change your world and cure your overwhelm.

I promise.

Believe it or not. And you may not.

Because the premise of this book is that **Overwhelm doesn't come from the external world . . . no matter how much you have to do and how many things you're juggling.**

You may be thinking that if I had any clue about your life and all you have to manage I could never -- would never -- say such a thing. But I'm saying it anyway.

Overwhelm is a mental thing.

An *internal* state.

You end overwhelm not by *doing* more or *doing* less but by internal shifts.

And you will learn how to make the necessary internal shifts by embracing and practicing certain steps that the End Overwhelm Now process will teach you, including:

1.   Understanding that overwhelm is a REACTION to the outside world, not caused by it. Trust me when I tell you that even with appearances to the contrary, overwhelm doesn't come from the chaos of the *outside* world. It comes from the chaos of your inner world: the space between your ears.

2.   Changing your thinking. For example, thinking that you have to do it all, that you have to do it now, that you have to do it "perfectly," that you have to do it alone, and that you'll *die* if you don't. Or that it's all too much or there isn't enough or you're not enough. This book will teach you how to replace those thoughts with the focused, organized thinking that keeps you at your best, helps you breathe again, and makes your world and your To Do list feel manageable. Changing your thinking will not only release you from overwhelm, but will also help you feel more empowered.

3. Changing your language. How you talk to yourself and the things you say are critical elements in how you create overwhelm in your life. Watch your language and watch things change.

4.   Shifting your attention. What you focus your attention on creates the minute-by-minute scenes and experiences of your life. Shift your focus and the scene shifts dramatically.

5. Changing your behavior. Aligning your behavior with your new thinking will support the feeling of empowerment. Give up the struggle to do more as the solution to your overloaded life. With the clarity that comes from new thinking and approaches, you will find that you can do less and be more effective.

The End Overwhelm Now Approach

The *End Overwhelm Now* process isn't a magical fix where you snap your fingers and things change overnight. Although the Emergency Intervention (Section II) can get you out of an overwhelm panic in about 20 minutes, permanently changing your pattern of becoming overwhelmed takes a little longer. However, it is a simple process that anyone can do. It absolutely works -- thousands of clients have proven this -- and it works quickly.

There are only a few key steps in breaking your pattern of overwhelm. They are **understanding** what is actually creating your sense of overwhelm, and then becoming aware of your **beliefs**, your **language**, your **attention** and your **behavior**. I'll teach you how to do all those things.

About This Book

End Overwhelm Now is divided into three sections. **Section I** is designed to teach you how to shift your patterns of thought and action so that you no longer become overwhelmed in your life . . . even if you have more to do than any human could possibly accomplish. You will gain an understanding of what overwhelm is, where it comes from, your role in creating it, and what it does to you physically and mentally. You'll learn why it's important to break your patterns; and, most important, you will learn how to make key internal shifts for ending your overwhelm.

Section II is an emergency intervention to use if you are overwhelmed right this minute. I didn't put it first because it's actually more important to do the more sustainable steps in Section I. In the emergency section, you'll find a step-by-step process to interrupt your state of overwhelm, restore you to sanity and -- in less than 30 minutes – move you into a more balanced and resourceful state. Use this section if you need to get yourself calmed down right now. Then, please go back and read Section I so you can learn the concepts that will *break your pattern* of constant overwhelm. A quick fix is great, but it doesn't solve the problem long term.

Section III shares stories of how people have put these principles into practice and succeeded in ending their pattern of overwhelm.

My Story of Overwhelm

Overwhelm was a natural way of life for me for many years. I was thrilled when I began working for a technology consulting company in 1989. I imagined the glamour of creating systems that would "wow" our Fortune 500 clients as I jetted around the world on "important business."

My new company prided itself on being able to do the impossible. In response to constant staff objections that there was too much to do and too little time, we often heard, "If it were easy, anyone could do it!" In my second month on the job, I was assigned to a demanding new project. Our Vice President advised us to tell family and friends that they shouldn't expect to see much of us for a while. He was right.

My dream of jetting around the world was shattered by years of a grinding commute, Sunday through Friday, from Denver to New York. My average day was 14 hours, spent with clients who could never be satisfied and deliverables that were always over-promised and overdue. My brief weekends home were spent doing laundry and reconnecting with my husband and family the best I could.

In 1995, the movie "Groundhog Day" was being shown on the plane, so every week, on my outbound flight, I watched Bill Murray re-live his own Groundhog Day, over and over. It felt a lot like my life, but at least he got a good night's sleep in between!

After 15 years of being a slave to deadlines, my company downsized, and I was one of the casualties. I had spent more than a dozen years accounting for where I was and what I was doing every minute of the day, and then my life suddenly flipped over. I had no direction, no obligations and . . . . no income.

So began a new life of finding my *own* goals, my *own* motivation, and my own direction. I had always been *told* what to do and was always busy fulfilling somebody *else's* goals. I realized that I had to trust myself to set my course instead of relying on an employer. I was excited, but the decisions I needed to make were overwhelming. When I started my own coaching business, there was so much at stake, and I feared making the wrong decisions. How to get clients? How to choose a website developer? What to do when the first website developer wasn't any good? I had more questions than answers. Instead of being overwhelmed by the strident demands of an employer, I was now overwhelmed by the process of birthing a new business.

I was determined to chart my own course and NOT live in the state of perpetual anxiety and overwhelm I had experienced for 15 years. It was imperative to learn how to still be a high achiever and perform to exceptional standards, but without the misery of constant overwhelm.

What I learned included the power of chunking the seemingly insurmountable mountain of tasks. I learned to ask for help and advice. I learned to leverage my small successes and accomplishments to create a sense of what I was capable of doing. I learned resilience: how to keep my courage up through the inevitable disappointments and setbacks. When that wave of thought and emotion that I called overwhelm threatened to stop me, I learned to intentionally redirect it to a more empowering meaning. I learned that my self talk was one of the most critical aspects of managing overwhelm. But the most important thing I learned was the process of changing my *thinking*. **Because overwhelm is a *state of mind* that *starts in the mind*.** And awareness of what is going on in our minds – what we are saying to ourselves – is everything.

As my coaching business grew, I had regular glimpses into other people's overwhelm. I started to see the patterns of those who were overwhelmed and, just as important, the patterns of those with tremendously busy, complicated lives who were *not* overwhelmed.

There wasn't a specific correlation between the length of the to-do list, or the financial capacity, or the intelligence and motivation of those who were overwhelmed, and those who weren't. Sure, having kids to raise and elderly parents and a demanding job and a home to take care of were often part of the overwhelmed person's life. But I also had the overwhelmed client who was a single student with plenty of money. Or the worker with a secure, manageable job and great family, who was overwhelmed anyway.

I began testing different psychological approaches to shift someone from overwhelm into empowerment within one coaching session. Section II, the Emergency Intervention, is the result of this testing process. But my goal was not just to help people get out of overwhelm in the moment. My ultimate goal is to show people – to show YOU - how to eradicate your own overwhelm. This book, and books and programs to come, are that solution.

The Beginning of the End

For a long time, I believed that a persistent feeling of overwhelm was something to be lived with, like a chronic backache or cranky neighbor. It seemed beyond my control, with my only option to somehow cope with its constant presence. However, when I learned how to **interrupt the pattern of overwhelm**, I learned that it IS possible to have a crazy-busy life AND live in a state of confidence, calm, peace, and empowerment.

Regardless of gender, culture, age, circumstances, or resources, my clients all experience overwhelm, much like I did. Sometimes their sense of overwhelm is from too much to do in a demanding environment, like in my consulting days. Sometimes it's from not knowing the next steps or doubting themselves, like my start-up days. Sometimes they're struggling with health problems, relationship challenges, and/or financial worries. The stories, strategies and tools in this book are the result of my work with myself and my amazing clients over many years. The strategies and tools I present have been tested with hundreds of people. I share them here so you, too, can end your overwhelm and create the life you want.

If you take just one message from this book, it is this: **You have the power to solve your overwhelm because – believe it or not – it is you (your mind) that creates it.** You have your own unique process by which you create your overwhelm in response to challenging tasks and situations. The great thing is that with awareness and practice, you can actually change your process and patterns. Like any other process of changing habits, it requires decision, commitment, awareness and practice, as well as having patience with yourself. The more you practice the strategies, the faster you will catch yourself and, ***eventually you will simply not feel overwhelmed anymore.***

This book will not only eliminate the stress of overwhelm, it will also ***enliven and empower your life.***

Are you ready to end your overwhelm now? Let's get started!

SECTION 1

Ending Overwhelm

Chapter 1

An Overview of Overwhelm

"To become different from what we are, we must have some awareness of what we are." ~ *Eric Hoffer, philosopher*

Why Am I So Overwhelmed?

If you want to stop living with your constant feeling of being overwhelmed, it is important to understand what overwhelm is and where it comes from. This section will arm you with a basic understanding of your overwhelm and help you recognize where you have the power to change it. Please read this section with an attitude of curiosity rather than blame or judgment. Your overwhelm reaction is not your fault and there's nothing wrong with you. In fact, you will come to learn how wise and resourceful you actually are.

The first step in understanding your overwhelm is realizing that we live in an unprecedented time with information and technology advancing faster than ever before. We enjoy many benefits, but are also crippled by overload. Nobody taught us how to manage it all. We're trying to figure out the new environment as fast as we can, and there are no right answers to those vast to-do lists.

So, yes, there are legitimate reasons why most of us experience overwhelm so much of the time.

Your Brain and Overwhelm

Although the world has been evolving at lightning speed, our brains have not. It has been 200,000 years since the human brain got its last major upgrade, which was the development of the prefrontal cortex. That evolutionary jump gave us tremendous reasoning capabilities. The prefrontal cortex gave us the ability to imagine and to perceive abstract concepts, which culminated in such advancements as language, money, and later, incredible leaps such as space travel and the internet.

The same prefrontal cortex capabilities that give us the ability to imagine and create new realities also give us a way to imagine and create our feelings of overwhelm. Because your brain's highest priority is keeping you alive, it will look for any threat to your survival. Look deeply enough, and you'll see that the foundation of overwhelm is *fear*. It may begin with a simple concern, such as disappointing someone, falling behind, or losing something. Or you may be facing a more significant threat, such as getting fired or not making enough money to pay the mortgage. Then you *amplify* that fear by focusing on the perceived danger, talking to yourself in disempowering ways, even imagining worst-case scenarios.

Studies of the brain show that anything vividly imagined creates the same responses in the mind and body as the real thing. As a result, your self-generated story creates the same physiological reaction our caveman ancestors experienced when confronted by a wild animal with big teeth and even bigger claws.

In our modern world, for the most part, those teeth and claws are in our imagination. We often don't recognize that we're scaring ourselves, but the fear is there. Blood pressure rises; energy is directed to the limbs; digestion and immune response are suppressed; and stress chemicals including cortisol and adrenaline flood your system to sharpen your senses and amplify your physical power to deal with the threat. Facing the possibility of death (i.e., any threat to survival, including the worry that you "can't get it all done"), your brain will do one of three things: Fight, Flight or Freeze.

- Fight: When an animal is threatened, it fights for survival. Sometimes a smaller weaker animal can intimidate a bigger aggressor by fiercely fighting back. Some people, when overwhelmed, become angry, aggressive or blaming. With that heightened physical reactivity, we lash out at the perceived threat (or innocent bystanders) by yelling, cursing or throwing insults. We also fight by taking some aggressive or protective action, which is generally not wise or well-planned.

- Flight: Another reaction to a threat is to run away. Many animals use their speed or agility to avoid danger. Humans don't physically run away from a fear reaction like overwhelm. Instead, we mentally and emotionally run away by distracting ourselves with something else that feels safer in the moment. We might do something inconsequential, but not what is most important or pressing. We have a wonderful euphemism for the flight response in our modern world: *procrastination*.

- Freeze: When an animal can't overpower or outrun the threat, it freezes, like the proverbial "deer in the headlights," uncertain about what to do next. In human terms, this is avoiding action entirely, what we call *avoidance* or *distraction*, such as binge-watching an old TV series, or medicating with food, alcohol, or drugs. We may even deny being in a disempowering pattern by giving an excuse for why we can't take action.

How do you react when you're overwhelmed? Do you choose fight, flight or freeze? In other words, do you tend to get aggressive, avoidant, or immobilized? Do you rely on a "crutch" like eating, smoking, or drinking alcohol to manage the feeling? It may be helpful to realize that your brain is simply trying to help you survive, given the situation you're perceiving. When you learn to change your perception of the situation, your brain no longer needs to run its ancient survival pattern.

How Overwhelm Is Different From Stress

Often when people are overwhelmed they refer to it as stress; however, there is an important difference between stress and overwhelm. Stress is a natural, physiological reaction that sometimes serves you. All animals experience stress when they're hungry or threatened. Presented with a real physical threat, the default reactions of fight, flight and freeze are absolutely necessary. Our ancestors' ability to react appropriately to stressors in their lives enabled us to survive and to evolve into the latte-drinking, screen-addicted achievers we are today. Some stress is actually beneficial. Known as "eustress," the physiological reaction we have to a small amount of stress is positive. It can make us more alert and improve performance. Stress responses are useful; and we wouldn't want to eliminate them. If an angry bear burst into the room, you would want your stress response to kick in. In the proper amounts -- and at the appropriate times -- stress can be beneficial.

What makes overwhelm different is that it's *self-inflicted*. And unlike stress, overwhelm *never* serves. As you'll learn in detail later in this book, overwhelm is *internally* generated through a pattern of thinking and behaving. Your amazing brain gives you the ability to create overwhelm, enlarge it, expand it, and sustain it for as long as you practice the pattern. Sadly, you can even make sure that it is with you all the time. It can become so chronic that we label it "stress," and assume there's nothing we can do about it. But because *your own controllable responses* are the actual culprit for your feelings of overwhelm, it is actually avoidable. Through your recognition of the patterns that create it, and your willingness to exercise the power you hold over it (the power you will gain by practicing the tools in this book) you will learn to end your overwhelm response to the challenges in your life.

And, as you will see in the next chapter, there are a number of important benefits to doing so.

Author's Note: There's an important distinction I want to make here. If you are feeling overwhelmed because you are in a truly health- or life-threatening situation, please seek the appropriate help. Yes, the tools in this book will help you to think more clearly about your situation and your options. But if you are in an abusive relationship, if you are abusing substances, or if believe your physical or psychological condition is chronic and health-threatening, please seek the attention of a trained professional. I've listed resources on my website to assist you.

Chapter 2

THE CASE AGAINST OVERWHELM

*"Every time you allow yourself to fall into the habit of being
overwhelmed; you steal a little from yourself and the world."*
~ Karen Van Cleve

Overwhelm does not serve us – not in any way. As we will
convincingly demonstrate in this chapter, it is only destructive and
has no productive or constructive elements whatsoever.

Overwhelm creates a fascinating lifestyle paradox; its impact
is **exactly the opposite of what we need most when we are
dealing with the complexities of life.**

The Paradox of Overwhelm

These are the ways that overwhelm is totally counterproductive:

* When we are overwhelmed, what we most need are
  resourceful solutions; but being in a state of overwhelm
  stifles the very resourcefulness we need.

* Feeling overwhelmed causes us to obsessively focus on
  external circumstances outside of us, which are often
  things we can't control. As a result, we miss the solution to

overwhelm, which is to focus internally on our strengths, priorities and actions.

- Overwhelm commonly triggers behaviors of distraction and procrastination. When the very thing we need is to focus, prioritize and take productive action, overwhelm has us do the exact opposite.

- When we're feeling overwhelmed, we neglect that which is most valuable and lasting. An example of this is neglecting our important relationships, or failing to act on what would make the most important and lasting difference. Indeed, if we focused on what was valuable and lasting, we wouldn't experience overwhelm.

- Shiny object syndrome: Our modern culture of distractions trains the brain to jump quickly from one thing to the next in response to each new stimulus. This response is especially active when we are in overwhelm as the next thing and the next thing grabs our attention in a distressing way. Eliminating overwhelm requires us to train our brains to intentionally focus on what we choose, directing our attention away from inconsequential things, whereas overwhelm exacerbates the shiny object response.

The paradox of overwhelm creates a cycle that becomes increasingly disempowering, which in turn increases the likelihood that we'll continue to repeat the cycle. It's like a deep hole: once we've fallen into it, and the more often we fall into it, the harder it is to get out. But get out we must.

Why We Must Break the Cycle

Don't con yourself into thinking that somehow feeling overwhelmed makes you or anyone else more motivated or productive. ***The exact opposite is true.*** Overwhelm is NEVER beneficial. It makes people feel *less* confident, *less* resourceful, *less* inclined to take action, *less* creative, and *less* resilient. This section will show you why you MUST take control of your cycle of overwhelm NOW.

Overwhelm is so pervasive today that it seems like a natural way of living. Maybe it's how you fit in with friends. Everyone is overwhelmed, so what's the big deal, right?

Wrong!

Here's why.

The Seven Critical Reasons to Do Whatever It Takes to Break Your Pattern of Overwhelm

Reason #1: Overwhelm Contributes to Chronic Stress . . . and Chronic Stress is Bad.

The mental churn, physical tension, and emotional turmoil of overwhelm create real negative impacts, including increased heart rate and blood pressure, altered thinking, difficulty sleeping, and suppressed immune response. The Centers for Disease Control estimates that the majority of doctor visits in the U.S. are stress related. In the American Psychological Association's 2012 survey, "Stress in America: Our Health At Risk," a significant percentage of respondents reported that their stress is increasing. Thirty-nine percent said their stress had increased over the past year, and 44%

said that their stress had increased over the past five years. Only 17% reported decreased stress in the past year. The trend is not encouraging. The chemicals released during stress suppress the immune system and are linked to increased illness (a 2012 survey showed people under chronic stress were more likely to catch the common cold), weight gain, slower healing, sleep dysfunction, heart disease, depression, ulcers and other stomach problems, as well as back and neck pain. (from AARP Bulletin, November 2014, *Stress! Don't let it make you sick*)

Reason #2: Overwhelm Impedes Decision-Making

The human brain isn't designed to process the vast array of options and opportunities available today. Just a century ago, the local general store might have stocked a total of 100 items. Now you have to choose from 100 varieties of cereal alone! Not to mention 800+ TV stations where there used to be four. Having too many options impedes effective decision-making.

You are making decisions from the moment you wake up until the time you fall asleep. For example, what to wear to work may seem like a simple question, but how many choices are there in your closet? And how does the weather impact your decision? Do you have to dress for any special meetings or events? What will others be wearing? Do you have an evening event to consider? What's clean? Even the most routine decision includes a number of factors. Now multiply that by the thousands of decisions you demand of your brain every day.

You may be suffering from "decision fatigue." The part of your brain that makes conscious decisions fatigues easily, resulting in a decline in the quality of decision-making. In studies of judges reviewing court cases, decision fatigue showed up in just a couple of hours. And guess what happens when the conscious brain fatigues? The unconscious mind goes for safety (i.e., "default"). That often means the choice that's the easiest to make, or no decision at all. The worst part about decision fatigue is that we don't realize when it's happening.

You may even find that you're overwhelmed *because* of all the decisions required. The best state for decision making is to strategically think about the outcome and rationally identify the possible courses of action. An overwhelmed mind doesn't think strategically or rationally. The focus is more likely on what you fear, rather than the outcome. One poor decision can cascade into self-doubt and second-guessing, which then often leads to the next poor decision.

Reason #3: Overwhelm Impacts Self-Esteem

When we're focused on so much to do and so little time to do it, we're setting ourselves up to "fail." We begin and end each day with an impossible to-do list. Or some of us are so intimidated by what we have to do that we're afraid to even write it down so we end up trying to manage without a written list. In either case, we tend to focus on what we *haven't* done instead of acknowledging the things we *have* accomplished, which contributes to the anxiety and powerlessness of overwhelm. Sadly, even when we have accomplished a great deal, many of us belittle ourselves for the things we didn't get done, or the one thing we screwed up or didn't do quite as well as we could have. We fail to celebrate, or even acknowledge, the 99 things we did well. This contributes to feeling bad about ourselves rather than confident, positive, empowered. Although in my practice it appears that women assume "there's something wrong with me" more often than men, both genders experience the pervasive, uncomfortable and disempowering feeling that the problem or lack is them – that if they were just more "something," they wouldn't find their life so overwhelming. The eroding of self-esteem is not only a negative consequence of allowing overwhelm to dominate our lives, it also contributes to feeling overwhelmed in the first place. So it's a vicious cycle, which we must find a way to interrupt if we want a happier life.

Once the pattern of overwhelm begins, it is self-perpetuating. Overwhelm is disempowering, so we take less action. This causes things to stay just as bad or get worse. So we spiral down even further by focusing on outside factors or dwelling on the past or ruminating on what we could or should have done.

Failure to act, or acting under the debilitating influence of overwhelm, starts to become – in our own minds -- a measure of who we are. There's a tendency to mentally stack one thing on top of another, building in our minds a mountain of problems and failed attempts. We forecast the future in colors as bleak as our present, or scare ourselves envisioning the worst-case scenarios. This cycle erodes our self-esteem even further and makes it that much harder to trust ourselves in the future.

Reason #4 to Break the Overwhelm Cycle: Overwhelm Diminishes Team Performance

Whether an organization places heavy demands on the staff or whether team members voluntarily take on excessive tasks, overwhelm can be considered a badge of honor in the workplace. In my last corporate position, it was expected that everyone would have more assignments than they could possibly complete.

If we weren't overwhelmed, we were seen as not very dedicated, even becoming known as "slackers." That culture encouraged unrealistic expectations and the fear of saying "no." However, *no individual, team or organization is ever more productive when operating in overwhelm*. Overwhelm triggers fear-based behaviors, like blame, information-hoarding, and lack of trust. As indicated above, it can also lead to diminished decision-making ability, which impacts performance. Overwhelmed employees lack the very perspective needed to invent new ways to handle their workload.

Reason #5 to Break the Overwhelm Cycle: Overwhelm Becomes a Cultural Norm

People who grow up in an environment steeped in overwhelm may not realize that there is another way to live. They assume "that's just the way it is." There can be a cultural competition for who is more overwhelmed, who is further behind or who is more oppressed by life conditions. In some strata of society, overwhelm becomes a badge of honor, even a way to fit in. Rather than a transient state, it becomes who we are and how we belong in the world. We're so conditioned to be overwhelmed that even if circumstances improve, we'll continue to be overwhelmed, even resisting the suggestions of others to let it go. Overwhelm has become a part of how we define ourselves and how we live.

Reason # 6: Overwhelm Becomes Habitual

We know that practicing an activity increases proficiency, and that whatever we practice repeatedly, and over time, becomes a habit. Unfortunately, the more you practice overwhelm, the more "natural" it becomes. In fact, you can "practice" overwhelm to the point that it becomes your brain's default response to any challenge or opportunity. It might even seem weird *not* to feel overwhelmed. I've worked with people who practice overwhelm even in their sleep. They wake up at 4:00 in the morning with the same thoughts churning over and over. The resulting mental and physical fatigue perpetuates the habit of overwhelm.

Reason #7 to Break the Overwhelm Cycle: Overwhelm is Contagious

If you spend a few minutes with someone who is immersed in overwhelm, you may find yourself caught up in it as well. The standard response to the greeting, "How are you?" is no longer a pleasantry like, "Fine." Instead, it's, "I'm *so* busy; my life is crazy." A natural reaction is to say, "Me too!" We exchange busy and overwhelmed stories. This commiserating can feel good; we've bonded with someone over shared challenges. But this only makes matters worse. Normalizing overwhelm perpetuates the cycle.

We are significantly influenced by what is happening with others. This is what Robert Cialdini, in his book, *Influence*, refers to as "social proof." He describes social proof as using "the actions of others to decide on proper behavior for ourselves, especially when we view those others as similar to ourselves." The more we're surrounded by those who are overwhelmed, the more likely we are to feel it ourselves. It's like that nasty winter cold that spreads rapidly. You don't want to pick up others' overwhelm, so be careful when you are exposed to it. Nor do you want to be a source of contagion. When you break the overwhelm cycle for yourself, you become the role model showing those around you another way to live.

Decide to Change Now

I included this section to help you realize why it is imperative to do whatever it takes to end your overwhelm. You deserve to live an empowered, fulfilled, happy life – not caught up all the time in fear-based reactions. Make the decision now to remove the pattern of overwhelm – and all its negative consequences – from your life. In the next chapter, you'll learn how to begin acting on your decision.

Chapter 3

THE PROBLEM IS NOT WHAT YOU THINK...
IT'S WHAT YOU THINK

"Things do not change; we change." ~ Henry David Thoreau,
philosopher, author

You may have started reading this book because you were hoping I would provide the "answer" for your overwhelm, that I had a magic pill that would be the solution for your problems. Or I'd tell you how to cut out the nonessential tasks in your life so you don't feel overwhelmed anymore. Or maybe you were hoping I will tell you how to manage your time better. Or learn to prioritize. Or learn to say no.

Many of us have been taught to look to the external world for answers. We have the illusion that if we just had the right time management system, we could manage it all. Or if we were more organized, or did the "right" things, we could keep up. But the fact is, there's neither the perfect time management system, nor enough time in our lives, to "do" our way out of overwhelm. Of course it's important to have a system for focusing, prioritizing and tracking tasks. But the idea that there is some external way to manage it all is an illusion. It distracts us from the only thing we can really manage, which is ourselves.

Now here comes the part of the book where I either lose you – and you continue your search for some other solution to your overwhelm – or you choose to stay with me and consider the possibility of a whole new approach.

Because here is where I lay out the radical premise of this book, which is simply: ***Overwhelm does not come from external circumstances; overwhelm is created internally.***

The problem of being constantly overwhelmed in your life is not what you think it is or where you think it is.

It's not the tasks, people, expectations, commitments, bosses, kids, house, co-workers, technology and endless to do lists.

Overwhelm is not a problem that comes from what's going on "out there."

Overwhelm is created in your mind. In the place between your ears.

 "Rubbish!" you may say, as you get ready to put this book down for good. Clearly I do not understand your life and all you are required to track, manage, and get done. Obviously I have no clue what your life is like.

Because if I understood the insurmountable challenges you face, I wouldn't make such a statement. If I understood how understaffed you are at work, or what your boss expects, or how little your partner helps out at home, or if the house didn't have constant maintenance problems, or you could find a reliable nanny or the traffic that slows your morning commute wasn't so unbearable or if your kid didn't need tutoring and you weren't trying to finish your MBA and working full time or if you didn't need to visit your mom every week and help her with her bills or figure out when to sell her house and get her into assisted living (which you will also have to research) and when are you going to fit in a workout or just some exercise, and get the car in for an oil change, and didn't have so many bills to pay and so little money, and your kid wasn't on the autism spectrum and needed so much supportive help and you didn't have to travel to Cleveland again this week and your admin wasn't on vacation the week before the board meeting and, and, and. . . . then you wouldn't for God's sake be so frickin' overwhelmed all the time.

And I totally understand your perspective. There was a time I would have heartily agreed with you.

But in working daily with people who are overwhelmed, I've been able to "see" inside the thinking that creates and sustains overwhelm. I've also been able to "see" inside the minds of people who successfully juggle vast numbers of responsibilities and tasks. As a result, I've developed a pretty good understanding of what I call the Dynamics of Overwhelm. And here's what I know: The Dynamics of Overwhelm are mostly centered around our thinking patterns and what we are saying to ourselves about our situation. I am not saying you don't have a lot to do. Even too much to do. More than any human could manage.

But what I am saying is that the state of overwhelm doesn't come from that.

It comes from the jabbering voice inside your head. From the voice that says that whatever you do isn't enough. Or that "other people" manage it all. It comes from waves of emotion: guilt, frustration, anger, confusion in response to the thoughts you're holding.

Ultimately, overwhelm comes from the stories you tell yourself, and how you react to those stories.

That may seem unbelievable to you in this moment with all you have to do and manage. But if you keep reading, I believe I will be able to clearly demonstrate to you that this is true.

Defining Overwhelm

My definition of overwhelm is this: *Overwhelm is a physical, emotional and psychological* **reaction** *to a pattern of beliefs, language, attention and behavior.*

In other words, in essence, **overwhelm is a reaction to how we are processing the outside world.**

A reaction.

Not caused by.

A reaction to.

A response.

Here's the good news: If it's a *reaction*, that means you have the power to control it. Because if you create it; you can un-create it. It means *you* hold the key to feeling so overwhelmed all the time. It also means you don't have to try to keep trying to control the outside world – which is hardly ever possible anyway. You just have to control what's going on inside your head. And I can teach you how to do that in a really effective way that will stop the pattern of overwhelm in your life.

Further good news: The simple power of awareness will begin the process of change all on its own.

Not that you don't have to DO anything.

You do.

But awareness alone starts the ball rolling in a very helpful way.

So, if you're willing to hang in here with me and open your mind to the possibility that this problem can be solved by shifting a few things *internally*, then you're ready to get started.

Just to clarify: there is no question that many of the clients I see – many of us – have VERY full plates. Overly full plates. Crazy lives. A mother of twin four-year-olds (one of whom needs speech therapy) with a demanding full-time job, two dogs, an old house, a sizable yard, an ailing mother-in-law, a husband she'd like to see every once in a while and no time to breathe let alone get to the gym or a yoga class – will tell me she is overwhelmed because, well, because *her life is overwhelming*.

And really, who can argue with that?

Well, umm, I can.

I can argue with that because I know – from years and years and years of experience coaching overwhelmed people – and from my own success at breaking my pattern of always feeling overwhelmed – I know without a doubt that even though her life is crazy full and crazy busy and crazy demanding, that her being overwhelmed is a *response* to her external circumstances. It's not caused by them.

And I know it because I often see people with similar lives and workloads and challenges. One of them is in a constant state of overwhelm and the other one – with basically the same amount of things to do – just isn't. To give you some real-world examples, I've included some client stories in Section III.

Hope

If it weren't true – that overwhelm is a state of mind, a *response* to what we have to manage, not caused by it – then everyone would have the same reaction to the same external circumstances. If it were not true, I surely could not have succeeded all these years in helping my clients NOT be overwhelmed by simply changing their thinking and patters. If it were not true, I could not have created a system that actually works for ending your state of overwhelm and written a book outlining the steps for doing so.

So if you can trust me a little further - trust that I am not a crazy person nor a person who just doesn't understand your life - but that I actually, just maybe, know what I'm talking about and just maybe can actually help you, then let's move on to understanding how the Dynamics of Overwhelm work their insidious and unhelpful ways in your poor brain.

Chapter 4

THE DYNAMICS OF OVERWHELM

"The primary cause of unhappiness is never the situation but your thoughts about it. Be aware of the thoughts you are thinking. Separate them from the situation, which is always neutral. It is as it is." ~ Eckhart Tolle, author

Once we accept the premise that overwhelm is an *internal* pattern of the mind, it becomes important to understand how the pattern works. There are two principal dynamics that sow the seeds of overwhelm and keep us held in its grip. Awareness of these mechanisms will help you understand specifically when and how overwhelm starts churning in your brain and will enable you to interrupt the cascade, thereby preventing the pattern from taking root so that overwhelm does not take over.

The principal dynamics of creating and perpetuating overwhelm are:

- Our **Beliefs**

- An interwoven combination of **Language, Attention and Behavior** which we refer to by the acronym **LAB**.

Beliefs

Beliefs Underlie Everything We Think and Do

A belief is a feeling of certainty that something (e.g., a thought) is true. Beliefs are pervasive, important and underlie much of our lives. We adopt beliefs from the moment we're born, based on what's modeled by the people around us and by our own experiences. We accumulate and shift our beliefs throughout our lives. Generally, we don't examine or question our beliefs. Yet they affect every aspect of our lives.

For example, when I was young, most women didn't work outside the home. If women did work, they were often teachers or secretaries. I believed those would be my options when I grew up, too. I planned to follow in my sisters' footsteps and become a secretary. I diligently practiced those skills. When I began my first job as a secretary, I discovered I was a *terrible* secretary. My belief in my future was shattered. Fortunately, my belief in my ability to learn and find a better match for my skill sets carried me through to a more successful career. If I had kept my belief that I *had* to be a secretary, I would have been unsuccessful and unhappy. The willingness to adapt and adopt a different belief freed me to pursue what was right for me.

Beliefs are not inherently good or bad. However, the impact of a belief on our thoughts, emotions and actions, and even our identities, can empower or limit us. There are three types of beliefs:

1) *A belief that is not true.* We're always discovering individual and global beliefs that aren't true. From Galileo's discovery that

the sun doesn't revolve around the earth, to the discovery as we mature that there is no tooth fairy or that our mom doesn't know everything, to personal discoveries – like me finding out that I wasn't meant to be a secretary -- truths that replace our previously held (untrue) beliefs reveal themselves throughout our lives.

2) *A belief that may be true but doesn't support you.* For example, the belief that you have a lot on your plate may be true, but it may not be supporting you right now so focusing on it may not be very useful. You may also believe that change is hard, and that you're not good at it. That may have seemed true in the past. But maintaining that belief will limit your future and result in a lot of struggle. A shift in perspective could be more useful.

3) *A belief that is true and also supports you.* For example, my belief that I could learn to be successful in another career. Another example might be to believe that you CAN learn and grow (because you've been doing that all your life). As a result, you can believe that YOU hold the solution to your overwhelm.

One of the key steps in ending your pattern of overwhelm, is to become aware of the beliefs you have, and to recognize which ones support you and which don't.

There are four main limiting beliefs that specifically contribute to, and even create, overwhelm. They trigger feelings of being out of control, and make us believe that the chaotic thinking that's making us crazy is based on things that are true. ***But they're not.***

These are **limiting beliefs** and they are hardly ever actually true. But we react to them as if they are both real and true.

These beliefs can show up individually or – as is often the case – in various combinations.

Limiting Belief #1: *If I Can't Keep Up, I'll Die*

Earlier I described the fight, flight or freeze fear reaction that occurs with overwhelm. This reaction to today's fast-paced, ever-changing world is rooted in our evolutionary history. Our ancestors had to keep up with their environments or die. If they didn't find or grow enough food, find shelter, find protection from predatory animals or warring tribes, they *could* die. The drive to keep up with our environments is a response wired into us from thousands of years of evolution.

We are the first generation faced with an environment evolving much faster than we can. Epigenetics shows that we're wired to biologically adapt to our physical environments in just one to two generations. (www.WhatIsEpigenetics.com)   However, it is no longer biological adaptation we need at this point.

We don't have an evolutionary adaptation for the scope and pace of our changing world. We have news from around the world all the time. More than one million books are published each year in the U.S. alone. We can socialize with people from around the world at all hours of the day. Even so, we still have the same nervous systems that our ancestors had. So when we can't keep up with our impossible environments, the ancient fear that served our ancestors is backfiring on us. Even if we tell ourselves intellectually that we aren't going to die, the instinctive feeling of panic is there.

What we need now is not biological adaptation, it's *psychological* adaptation that we urgently require to deal with the pace of change.

The psychological adaptation we need in regard to today's environment is a belief shift. We need to find a way to wire in the understanding that if we do not keep up with our environment – with our to-do lists, with technology, with the news, with politics, with the Kardashians, with the newest Google algorithms, with the NYT best seller list, with our friends on Facebook, with downloading the newest version of Windows, with the kids' sports or homework, with the laundry, even with the top sales guy at work -- **we will not die**.

Not even close.

Despite the fact that that response is wired into us from millions of years of evolution, **it is not true**.

For me, survival worry was as recent as my parents. They were children during the Great Depression during which there were real risks of not getting enough -- food, fuel, heat, shelter, ration cards – to survive. My father served in Europe during World War II, where he could die any day from a number of dangers. These were real life-threatening circumstances. My own life was not plagued by either the Depression or the War. However, for much of my life, I had the feeling that if I couldn't keep up in school, or keep up in the workplace, or be a perfect family and community member, or get things just right, that the world would come to an end . . . that I might die.

Fortunately I now recognize that is an ancient impulse *that is simply not true*. With the important recognition – that the *I Might Die* thought was underlying my discomfort *and it was not true* -- I have learned to re-wire that belief/response and circumvent the feelings of overwhelm and panic it engenders. And I have taught my clients how to do the same.

You can't imagine the difference it makes.

In the Overcoming Overwhelm chapter, you'll learn how to interrupt and calm your own evolutionary reaction rooted in "If I don't keep up, I might die." What is most important now is that you recognize that this ancient pattern may be contributing to, or even causing, your overwhelm.

Limiting Belief #2: *It's All Too Much*

You're at the mercy of this overwhelm trigger when you have a long to-do list, whether it's composed of things you have to do, should do or even want to do. You mentally churn through the list over and over. Or maybe you don't even have a list; you look around and see everything you need to do or should be doing and become overwhelmed by the magnitude of it all.

With the belief that it is all too much, it is nearly impossible to function. If it's all too much and there is no possible way to do it, why would you even get started? Why would you attempt it? Clearly it is a losing battle. Letting the "It's all too much" belief pattern take hold ensures you will be unable to function in an effective way. It's a form of overwhelm almost guaranteed to shut you down. And, as the gotta-do's, oughta-do's, worries and problems stack up on one another, at some point, your mental state is going to collapse.

Limiting Belief #3: *There's Not Enough*

You're at the effect of this trigger when you are focused on what you don't have. You don't have enough time to do it all, or enough money to take care of it, or enough people (family, friends or help) to support you. Lack and scarcity is also an evolutionary fear that is often out of place in our modern, over-abundant world. This trigger often shows up in combination with the "It's too much" trigger. When we're focused on what we don't have, we are tripped into overwhelm more quickly.

Limiting Belief #4: *I'm Not Enough*

You're at the effect of this trigger when you are focused on what you lack as a person, when you focus on your shortcomings or on what's wrong with you. You might tell yourself, "I'm not smart enough," "young enough/old enough" "organized enough," etc. This trigger also shows up as labels you give yourself, such as "I'm a procrastinator." You may feel guilty for not doing everything you think you "should" be doing. Or you may be chasing the ever-elusive "perfect" result. The "I'm-not-enough" trigger is amplified by comparisons, especially unrealistically comparing yourself to others you see as successful. The larger the gap you see between yourself and the needs of your situation, the greater your feeling of overwhelm will be.

Recognizing How the 4 Limiting Beliefs Show Up For You

Although you'll learn strategies to manage these Belief Systems (BS) in the "Overcoming Overwhelm" chapter, just beginning to recognize and notice these patterns of thinking will allow you to "see" what's happening in your own mind.

Take a minute to notice your own responses as you start feeling overwhelmed. How do you generally feel and what words can you catch that you usually use to describe your overwhelm?

- There's so much coming at me; it feels like I'm buried.

- There's never enough time, money, or opportunity.

- Everyone else seems to have it under control.

- What's wrong with me? Why can't I handle this?

- I feel guilty/angry/frustrated/sad because I can't get it all done.

- It's all too much! I wish I could just run away.

- I feel so out of control.

- I have to take care of so many others (boss, spouse, family, friends).

- I don't know how to get out of this situation, or problem....

- It seems like it will be this way forever.

- I feel sick (or tired or sad or frustrated, or _____) when I think about all I have to do.

- I don't even know where to start.

- I have *so* much to do that I don't or can't do *any* of it.

- No matter how hard I try or how fast I go, I never catch up.

Starting to notice the disempowering beliefs that kick in when you're feeling overwhelmed is an important step in learning to interrupt your particular pattern.

LAB: Language, Attention and Behavior

Beliefs are the underlying, but not the only, mechanism that creates and sustains chronic overwhelm. We each create our unique pattern of overwhelm with a specific intertwined pattern of Language, Attention and Behavior – which we refer to by the acronym "LAB."

Here's how LAB works:

- We are constantly deciding what to pay attention to . . .

- while running a constant and incessant inner dialog . . .

- which reinforces what we're paying attention to . . .

- and then triggers a pattern of behaviors in response.

The three elements of *Language, Attention* and *Behavior* interact in a variety of different ways with an interwoven and often cascading effect. Sometimes our language triggers what we are paying attention to or our attention triggers our behavior or our behavior triggers our language or our language directs our attention.

The three intersecting dynamics of Language, Attention and Behavior are critical for learning how to end overwhelm so it is important to understand each of these elements.

Language:

What You Say to Yourself Matters

When I was a kid, my mom taught me a little saying to protect me against bullies. You probably learned it too. "Sticks and stones may break my bones, but words can never hurt me." That sentiment may deflect a bully, but your nervous system doesn't buy it. Because words can, in fact, hurt you. You are very much impacted by words, and most especially by the *words you say to yourself* -- both *what* you say and *how* you say it.

When you're overwhelmed, your internal dialog is quite different than when you are feeling strong or relaxed.

To interrupt your pattern of overwhelm, we will teach you how to notice what you say to yourself and to others that helps create or deepen your overwhelm. And we'll teach you how to talk to yourself in a different and empowering way that diffuses feeling of overwhelm. You'll also learn how to change your language patterns to prevent overwhelm from developing in the first place.

Attention:

What You Focus On Helps Create and Amplify Overwhelm

Every minute of your day is impacted by what you choose to focus on as well as what you *don't* focus on. You can pay attention to everything that's going wrong, or focus on what's going right. You can try to think about absolutely everything you have to do as if it all must be done NOW, or you can focus your attention on completing the next important task, and then the next. Or focus on solving a problem instead of wanting to avoid it. Your ability to choose what to pay attention to plays a huge role in managing – and eventually avoiding altogether – your sense of overwhelm. This isn't "learn to look at the bright side" advice. What I teach is a significant shift in how to process your reality.

BEHAVIOR:

Your Actions Are Impacted By -- And Often Contribute To -- Your Overwhelm

When overwhelmed, many people move into a kind of paralysis where they avoid doing anything, or avoid doing the most important things. For example, distracting ourselves with social media is a common behavior in the face of overwhelm. This pattern of behavior is not only counterproductive, it perpetuates the cycle of overwhelm because the lack of meaningful action results in feeling even more overwhelmed. Another reaction to overwhelm is the frantic, multi-tasking whirlwind that feels like progress, but leaves you feeling mentally, emotionally and physically spent ... and *still* having too much to do.

Aristotle said, "We are what we repeatedly do." Failure to take action, or taking hyperactive action, becomes self-perpetuating, and can ultimately affect how we see ourselves. Behavior, braided with Language and Attention, reinforces itself in a downward spiral of increased overwhelm and feelings of powerlessness. In the Solutions section, you will learn how to take action so that what you do – your behavior - minimizes or prevents overwhelm.

An Example of LAB in Action

Every one of us is using our LAB patterns all the time. When we're overwhelmed it's because of the particular ways that we use our language, attention and behavior. Change the pattern, and you change how you feel, ending up in a more resourceful and empowered state --*resourceful* and *empowered* being the exact opposite of feeling overwhelmed.

Here is a useful illustration of how LAB is the underlying operating system creating the overwhelm response. In this example, the *external* circumstances of the two gentlemen are quite similar, which helps makes very clear how it is the *internal* response – and in particular each one's LAB – that makes the difference.

Although these are real clients and real situations, these are not their real names.

Bryan and Garrett have similar businesses. Bryan has been losing sleep worrying that his finances and business seem out of control. His worry and lack of sleep mean he is not in a resourceful or confident state from the start. Facing a meeting with an important client, his mind goes in circles about the last time they met, which he labels as "disastrous." He keeps replaying the presentation in his mind. Bryan focuses over and over on what he should have done differently. He could have had an open and honest conversation with the client about his concerns, but he was too afraid. So he distracted himself with other activities. As the meeting approaches, he can't help thinking about his financial obligations and how "devastating" it would be to lose this client. How would he even start to replace him? If he loses this client, he might not be able to pay his mortgage, then where would he be? Leaving for the meeting, he feels totally overwhelmed and unsure of himself. The desperate voice in his head says, "You better not screw this up," as he walks into the meeting.

Garrett also runs his own business and is concerned about his company's financial situation. In response, he has started putting a new marketing plan in place. Facing a meeting with an important client, he also remembers the previous meeting in which he didn't get the deal or the "yes" he had hoped for. Garrett reviews the meeting to learn what he might have done differently or better, but doesn't obsess over it. He also understands that, since it happened in the past, there's nothing he can do to change it. He chooses to put his focus on the value he knows his product delivers and how best to communicate that to the client in a compelling way. While researching the client's current circumstances, Garrett discovers a new area where his product has a helpful application. He feels enthusiastic and confident about adding that to his presentation. He needs the revenue from this client to meet his financial obligations, but reminds himself that he is developing a marketing plan for new business. Leaving for his meeting, Garrett feels excited about the possibilities and pretty confident that the client is going to like his ideas.

Both men are facing similar situations, but Garrett's pattern of language, attention and behavior helps him enter the meeting with optimism and confidence. He is proactive and resourceful, rather than passive and reactionary. Both men might be anxious because each meeting is important, but Bryan's self-talk (using words like "disastrous" and "devastating"), his focus on what is wrong rather than what is possible, and his avoidance behaviors escalated legitimate concern (or even "pressure") into feeling overwhelmed.

Garrett's focus, self-talk and proactive behavior turned his nerves into positive anticipation rather than negativity and overwhelm.

This may seem like a very simplistic example. It might even look like I'm preaching a Pollyanna, "focus on the positive" mentality, but I assure you I am not. I am attempting to illustrate that what we choose to focus on, the words we use to talk to ourselves, and the actions we do and do not take, make all the difference when operating in our world.

To develop awareness of how LAB functions in your own life, take a minute to think back to the last time you were overwhelmed in a specific situation.

- **Language:** What did you say to yourself? Did you use language that amplified your concerns? Did you call yourself names or catastrophize the situation? Did you ask questions that took you into a mental dead-end, or questions that helped you be resourceful?

- **Attention:** What were you paying attention to? Were you focusing on what was going wrong, or what was great? What future scenarios were you imagining? Were you focused on the fear or on the possibilities?

- **Behavior:** What did you do as a result of your language and attention? Did you take confident strong action, or did you respond with fight, flight or freeze?

As you become aware of your LAB patterns in your own life and work to shift them (which we'll teach you in the next section) you will immediately start to see a significant shift in how "overwhelming" your life feels to you.

Chapter 5

OVERCOMING OVERWHELM: OVERRIDING LIMITING BELIEFS

"What we can or cannot do, what we consider possible or impossible, is rarely a function of our true capability. It is more likely a function of our beliefs about who we are."
~ Tony Robbins, author and Peak Performance Strategist

The previous chapters gave you an understanding of the origins of the overwhelm response, the many reasons it would be beneficial to end overwhelm in your life, and the dynamics and mechanics of how overwhelm operates.

In this chapter, I will give you the tools for gaining control over your overwhelm and regaining control over your life.

This section includes tools for combatting each of the unhealthy dynamics that lead to overwhelm. You certainly don't have to use them all . . . that could be overwhelming! What I encourage my clients to do is to start with the ones in which they most easily recognize themselves – *"Yeah, that's me; I definitely think that, do that, say that"* -- and then experiment with others later on.

None of the tools are difficult or time consuming; and with patience, practice and persistence the shifts they engender actually become a natural response. If you practice enough, new patterns (and neural pathways) are created and your new responses begin to automatically shut off or reroute the overwhelm response.

Recently I watched this in action when I was feeling overloaded and stressed prior to leaving town. It was almost as if -- from years of practice -- as the tendency toward overwhelm started to build, a circuit breaker flipped and just rerouted me to more calm, clear and resourceful thinking. My clients report the same phenomenon. Eventually, it's not that they have to keep using the tools to talk themselves down from overwhelm; it's more that the pattern has actually been interrupted and the processes they've learned seem to head overwhelm off at the pass.

That's what you have to look forward to.

For now, I'm going to teach you how to interrupt the pattern of each of the Dynamics of Overwhelm one by one.

How To Overcome Erroneous Belief #1: *If I Can't Keep Up, I'll Die*

When the psychological and physiological response of *"I'm Going To Die"* hits, it can happen suddenly. For some people, it's a racing heart, churning mind, powerful emotions, or all three. My client Dean often woke up at 2:00 a.m. with his mind spinning with worry, speculation and catastrophizing. Although his rational mind recognized that he was safe and not in any true danger, his nervous system was on life support.

There are several ways to calm your inner caveman:

For physical reactions: Your body has a physiological response to the belief that you are in danger and that death may be imminent.

As we've discussed in the previous chapter; the physical response is there from thousands of years of evolution, which CAN be overcome through intention. Your aim here is to overcome the wired response by consciously triggering a **relaxation response.** There are multiple ways to calm your body, and they take very little time:

- Nature provides a remedy -- always at hand -- for our physiological stress response: the breath. Taking several slow, deep, intentional breaths automatically begins the relaxation response. This is the same mechanism that causes us to spontaneously take and release a deep breath when we finish something important, or when we walk out of work after a long day. *Our bodies know how to relax when we allow them to do so.* When you find yourself caught up in overwhelm, stop for a moment and take four deep breaths. Inhale deeply through your nose for five seconds, filling your lungs as fully as possible. Hold for three seconds, then exhale through your mouth for five seconds. You may even want to make either an "ooooh" sound or an "aaaaah" sound as you exhale. See if you can empty your lungs before taking the next slow, deep breaths. **Those 4 breaths will take about one minute and will significantly alter your body's tense state.** Trust your intuition if you feel you need a few more breaths to center yourself.

- As crazy as it sounds, smiling or laughing also helps to trigger your relaxation response. In research studies, smiling even for no reason, increases people's perceptions of feeling more relaxed and happy. I have a friend who, when she is freaking out in traffic and knows it's going to make her late, will tune her radio to the 24/7 comedy channel. The traffic doesn't go away and she may still be late for the appointment, but her mind, body and emotions are no longer reacting as if she is going to die if she can't get off the highway and to her meeting on time.

- See if you can identify exactly *where* you're holding on to tension, or where there's some other physical reaction to overwhelm. Are your shoulders so tense they are up visiting your ears? Is there an uncomfortable feeling in the pit of your stomach, or is your heart racing? Take a moment to notice, and then consciously acknowledge and release the tension, or simply be present with what you're feeling in your body. We tend to resist what we're feeling, which ultimately makes us hold on to it longer. There is such wisdom in the body; taking a moment to connect with the physical sensations may provide insight or a message to help you.

- The right music can also help to free you from the reaction of overwhelm. In 1697 the poet William Congreve wrote, "Music has charms to soothe a savage breast," and that remains true today. Research shows that music has the ability to interrupt our psychological and physiological reactions to stress and overwhelm. (http://www.ncbi.nlm.nih.gov/pmc/articles/ PMC3734071/)

For the *psychological* reactions to *I'm Going To Die*: Once the body has been calmed down, here are the tools for addressing the psychological aspects of the feeling that you could die by not keeping up.

- **Ask yourself what you're really afraid of.** Determine if there is any real risk or danger to you right now. Almost always, the answer is no. Although the monster under the bed and the boogeyman in the closet are overused clichés, they are appropriate here. When I was a child, I sometimes convinced myself that there was a monster hiding in my room. The more I imagined the monster, the more details I invented in my mind; he got bigger, with sharper teeth, longer claws, even nasty matted hair. The more vividly I imagined him, the more real he seemed. As soon as I turned on the light, though, the monster disappeared. Similarly, when we're ruminating on what went wrong in the past or scaring ourselves with imaginings of the future, we need to turn on the light of awareness and check in with ourselves to identify the real fear.

Sometimes the light of awareness reveals that there is no life-threating fear and sometimes it does us the great favor of helping us realize what our fear really is – and then we can deal with it. Matt was overwhelmed by what seemed like a failed job search. Although he had valuable skills and experience, interviews were not turning into job offers. Matt worried that he was facing a career dead-end. The more he worried, the less energy he had, the less confidence he felt, and the more he procrastinated on taking action. He feared that he wouldn't be able to support his family if he didn't find a job.

Matt attended a seminar that helped to reveal some underlying beliefs. As he started understanding himself better, Matt realized that he didn't want to be an employee. He developed a brilliant idea for a website that fully utilized his strengths: his industry knowledge and years of experience. Once he was more aligned with what he really wanted, instead of what he thought he "should" be doing, Matt's energy was unleashed. He took powerful, focused action to create the business of his dreams. The real solution couldn't be identified while Matt was immersed in his fear about the job and his resulting overwhelm.

- **WAM–It**: In the year 60 A.D., the Roman philosopher, Seneca, offered one of my favorite overwhelm quotes: "There are more things that frighten us than injure us, and we suffer more in imagination than in reality."

I appreciate Seneca's quote as a reminder that, as humans, we create our own imaginings of things that will never happen. So another way to break your psychological fear response is to use a tool I invented called WAM-it. You can find a formatted document on the website, but it's easy enough to create for yourself. Think about the situation that's most triggering the feeling that you're going to die. Maybe it's the feeling you can't keep up, or you can't do it perfectly, or someone will get mad, or you'll lose your job. To illustrate, I'll use the example of Shawn's worry about delivering an important project a few days late.

On a sheet of paper, draw 2 vertical lines to create three columns.

In the first column, list your W's: your worries or "what-ifs" related to this situation. List anything that comes to mind, even (or especially) if it seems trivial or silly. Sometimes those are the worries that create the greatest overwhelm. In the middle column -- "the A" column -- for every Worry, list any ways you can Avoid or prevent that occurrence. In the third column, the "M" column, for every Worry, list the ways to Mitigate or Manage the occurrence, even if it does happen.

Here's Shawn's example:

W Worry or What-if	**A** Avoid or Prevent	**M** Mitigate or Manage
I can't finish the necessary analysis in time	Who on my team can help with the analysis? How can I use past successful analysis efforts to creatively speed this one up?	I'll keep my manager updated so s/he knows about the risk.
I'll have to do poor quality work to meet the deadline	Is there a way to reduce the scope, to do it in phases, or to get someone's help?	What's the real risk of "poor quality?" What are the most important parts to do really well, and what can I let slide a little? I'll deliver the work as "preliminary" and offer to deliver a more thorough job in the future.
The project will be late and I'll get fired	I'm doing a great job on everything else, this isn't so important they'd really fire me. How do I add meaningful value to the company?	If I did get fired, what's the worst that would really happen? Where would I begin with looking for another job? What would be great about being unemployed?
The project will be late and the client will be mad	How can I make sure the client gets what they really need by the deadline?	What would be the consequences to the client? How could I still be helpful and keep them happy, even if the project is late? How could I negotiate an extension, or offer to deliver in phases? What could I do to apologize and help them feel we still value them?

You'll be surprised, first, at how many things you're worried about. Then you'll be surprised that you can develop potential strategies to handle the list you've created. This exercise also highlights when you're worried about something outside of your control, because the best you can do is Manage it. See the "Attention" section below for more on the topic of focusing on things outside your control. For example, the client being mad as a reaction to the late report is outside Shawn's control.

How to Overcome Limiting Beliefs #2, #3 and #4

Beliefs #2, #3 and #4 of the overwhelm-triggering Limiting Beliefs are:

It's All too Much

There's Not Enough

I'm Not Enough

These three often show up together in what I call a "**Stacking and Lacking**" pattern. They're often interrelated, and have us focusing on both *too much* and *too little* (very crazy-making) so it makes sense to begin by dealing with them as a group.

The strategy for overcoming these dynamics starts with taking the time to identify which of these triggers is at work when you are overwhelmed or even when you first feel overwhelm starting to build.

Take 10 seconds to stop to discern which of the three are in operation – or which two or maybe all three – to clearly identify what is in play. *This step alone can make a significant* *difference in your state.* Sometimes, just consciously identifying the triggering beliefs can shift our response because listening and discernment itself moves us from crazy, overwhelmed mind into rational mind.

Once you have identified which belief is running the show, I recommend saying it out loud so you can hear yourself. For example, say out loud, "I believe am not enough." This helps you clearly single out what is creating your feeling of being overwhelmed. Then take whichever one is plaguing you (or more than one) and work with each one as follows:

The Disempowering Belief that It's All Too Much

The first step is to get the "too much" into manageable form. In a way, your mind telling you "it's all too much" is actually correct. Because your brain can only hold from three to seven things in active memory before it becomes overwhelmed. An example of this is when someone tells you numbers you are trying to memorize; you'll easily remember the first few numbers, but generally by the fifth or sixth number, you start to have some trouble. When you're stressed or overwhelmed, the number of things your brain can comfortably manage and retain is even lower. So your impossibly lengthy to-do list with multiple priorities is guaranteed to overwhelm you.

When you're in "It's All Too Much" mode, you have to give your brain a break. . The BIG list is causing you to feel near the "It's All Too Much" breaking point, so we have to get that list manageable for your brain. We're going to do that by taking a few minutes – that's all it takes -- to list the FEW most important things that are weighing on you Here are the steps in the process:

1) Begin by asking yourself the question: **"What SPECIFICALLY is most causing me to feel overwhelmed *right now*?"** This is not your to-do list; these are the *few things* that are causing you to feel overwhelmed. Most people list four to seven causes before their minds go blank for a moment. You may be tempted to add more to your list because there's so much going on in your head, but to end your cycle of overwhelm in the moment, you only have to address the few things that came up as your first answer to the question.

- **Be *very* specific.** Make sure you're identifying specifics, not vague generalities. Don't write down "work" or "my job." Write, instead, "the Smithson proposal" or, even better, "developing the spread sheet for the Smithson proposal" or "the market research section of the Smithson proposal." Don't write "school;" write specifically "the upcoming term paper in my psychology class." If the specific item is too big, that *alone* can contribute to your overwhelm because it's too big, vague, or complex for your brain to grasp.

2) Next, look at the list and see if you can **identify the one thing** that would free up the most energy for you. Yes, it's all got to get done and it's all important, but **is there one thing on the list troubling you the most?** Because when you identify this item, you will notice a pretty significant shift. Renee, whose story you will read as an example in Section II was facing finals week in her second semester in medical school. She had only three days left to prepare for a mind-spinning list of finals, papers and presentations. It was all important, all urgent, and way too much for her tired mind to juggle. At some point in our session, we were able to uncover that while every single element was big and concerning, the thing causing her the most concern and anxiety was a presentation that

she was dreading. Because she didn't know what the instructor was going to ask that might put her on the spot, the presentation felt out of her control. We separated that item out from the list and created some strategies for helping her be more confident and prepared. All she *could* control was herself: how she prepared and how she showed up. This action alone --*turning her attention to what was bothering her most and giving it some focused attention* --provided her with more peace of mind.

3) Next, for each item on your overwhelm list, think of just the next **one to two small steps** you could take to resolve or move each of those most important items forward, even just a little. *They must be small steps.* If they're large tasks, break those down into the first few small steps, or micro-actions. Don't write: "clean the house before the in-laws arrive" say, "clean the guest bath." **Write those steps down.** This helps you identify *concrete and do-able* steps to resolve the emotional and mental swirl of overwhelm. You have also engaged the logical, executive thinking part of your brain to create a plan. If there's no action you can take, **notice if that item is even within your control.** If it's something you can't control (e.g., someone else's behavior), identify what you *can* control or influence to manage the situation, and put that on your list.

4) Next, figure out specifically when and how those few small tasks will be completed. Ask for help from someone, or schedule a specific date and time that you can commit to taking care of the tasks that are most contributing to your overwhelm. You can also decide to intentionally delay (push it out to a future date) or to drop it (choose not to do it at all). Although there may be consequences to delaying or dropping a task, they may be more manageable than your persistent stress of carrying it on your list.

- If there's anything else on the list that you can do quickly, take care of it now and **acknowledge yourself** for organizing the overwhelm chaos into a plan. Action begets action. And action dispels the "it's all too much" myth because taken one thing at a time, you realize, it's do-able.

When you take the time to go through these steps you'll still have a lot on your plate, but you will begin to see that you can't do it all at once anyway. *All you can ever do is one step at a time.* And the smaller each of those actions is, the more momentum you can gain because with each thing you do, you get to watch your overwhelm list diminish. In the process, you may notice that your breathing has changed, that your shoulders have dropped from where they were hanging onto your ears and that maybe your mind feels a little clearer and your life a little more manageable. When you hear yourself saying, "It's all too much" take a second to counteract it and remind yourself, "Not, it's really not; I've got the important things organized now in a way I can handle."

The Disempowering Belief that There's Not Enough

Your first task here is to ask yourself quite frankly, *"Is this true?"* Is there really not enough time, enough money, enough knowledge, enough resources for what you **really must** get done? If the answer is *Yes, it's true*, then you will need to stop and make a *realistic* Plan B. If there's really not enough time to stop at the office for the file and get to the meeting on time, or to get to the store before picking up the kids from daycare, or to get the Smithson proposal done and fit in the meeting with the Palmers, then make a different plan or make new arrangements. If there's not enough money to hire a marketing person and a social media expert, if you really don't have enough knowledge to create sophisticated graphs from the Excel spread sheet, if you really don't have enough money for granite on the counters *and* the island, then STOP, recognize the reality of the limitation of whatever resource is scarce and create a workable solution. Trust me, there is one. It might not be your ideal scenario, but there is a workable solution. No one is going to die.

Often however – most often if I may go out on a limb and say so – "there's not enough" isn't really true. It feels that way, yes, but it's not actual fact. Often there *is* enough, but our brains create a panic situation by focusing on lack. This is a very basic survival mechanism. We focus on what's wrong, not what's right; on what there might not be enough of rather than what there is plenty of; on the ways we're in danger, not the ways we're safe. It has kept us alive for thousands of years, but it's not a good strategy for living in today's world.

Sandy lamented that she didn't have enough time. I asked her what specifically she didn't have time to do. This took her by surprise. She had felt a lack of time for so long, she didn't remember exactly why it was an issue. She thought for a moment, and said that she didn't have enough time to do the things she enjoyed. Again, I asked what specifically she wanted to have time to do. Sandy provided a few ideas for what she wanted to do, including some travel. When we got really specific about the activities, she realized she didn't have the money or the vacation time to do *everything* she wanted to do anyway. So we talked about how she could space out the activities, and enjoy planning for each one as part of the experience. As we talked about a timeline for all the fun things Sandy wanted to do, she got excited about the process. She then realized that she could use time as a resource (planning her fun activities over time) instead of feeling that she didn't have enough time *today* for all of it.

One way to reassure yourself that there *is* enough is to make a list of the resources available to help with the things that seem overwhelming. When we're overwhelmed, we tend to *isolate*; to get out of overwhelm, it helps to *collaborate*. Use the space and the examples below and **take just one or two minutes to create your own list of resources**. These may include:

- People you know who can offer a) information you need, b) encouragement or emotional support, c) connections to other people or resources, d) talents or abilities you need.

- Specific knowledge or skills needed. Where could you learn what you don't know? Who could help you learn what you believe you lack? Who could you hire who already has this knowledge or skill?

- Financial resources. If you perceive money to be an obstacle, how much do you realistically need, and what are a few options for financial support? If you freed yourself up from limiting beliefs about the lack of money, or what people are or aren't willing to do to support you, what would be possible? How could you learn more about how the people who started with nothing and created wealth, and how they did it?

- Time resources. If you perceive time to be an obstacle, what activities or commitments can you delegate, delay, or dump? Which are the most important, and why? What are some ways to speed up even some parts of your tasks? What do you tell yourself about time that amplifies your stress about time?

- The internet: For the first time in human history, the answer to just about any question or problem you might have is accessible via the internet. There's a YouTube video to teach you, a directory of expert resources, email to send out an SOS call. If you're feeling like it's all you all alone, remember than someone accessible via the web has figured out something similar.

If you can't come up with any resourceful ideas yourself, make an appointment to brainstorm this list with someone else who can see the situation more objectively than you can right now.

The Disempowering Belief that I'm Not Enough

When you focus on your lack of knowledge or expertise; being the wrong age (either too old or too young); having inadequate education, credentials or experience; and/or comparing yourself to others who may have more of the perceived qualities you think you are lacking, you are setting yourself up for the powerlessness that is overwhelm.

Because, really, what can you do about any of these now in your present situation? You can't be a different age, have different experiences, have studied something else in college, or be as young, old, smart or experienced as either Jordan or Julia. All you can do by focusing on what you lack (which most of the time is imaginary anyway) is to feel powerless and paralyzed.

I'm Not Enough and Emotions

Notice your emotions when you believe you're not enough. None of them are helpful. Guilt is common followed closely by frustration, anger, anxiety, hopelessness, sadness and others. We tend to have a "default emotion" that we revert to automatically when we're overwhelmed, so I enjoy challenging my clients to a "fast" or a "cleanse" with their primary I'm Not Enough emotion. For example, if you tend to feel guilty because you can't be everywhere at once - caring for your children, working, and being at the gym – experiment with letting go of your guilt for two weeks. When guilt pops up, remind yourself, "No, I'm not doing guilt this week." Choose to feel determined, or hopeful, or enthusiastic instead. Something else besides guilty. Remember, you have the power to choose your reactions to your outside world, including your emotions. At the end of two weeks, if you really want to go back to feeling guilty, and if it serves you, feel free to have your guilt back. This process works just as well for any disempowering emotion, not just guilt.

Similarly, many of us have a "bully" voice that beats us up when we're not as ___ as we "should" be (e.g., not as productive, organized, efficient, patient, you-name-it). That bully never lets us win, and never lets us rest. It tells us we "should" be taking better care of the kids when we're at work, and pay more attention to work when we're with the kids. Not letting ourselves "win" (feel successful), no matter what, also contributes to the feeling that we're not enough. For more on this topic, see the section below entitled "The Bully Voice."

The Fix for I'm Not Enough

When we're overwhelmed, we tend to see our challenges as bigger than they really are, and ourselves as smaller and less capable than we really are. The to-do list is huge, the problems are frightening, and we focus on our struggles and failures more than our successes. To end the overwhelm that comes from "I'm not enough," you must flip this around. The way to do that is to remind yourself, in a deliberate and conscious way, of your strengths and capabilities.

Although it might be the last thing you want to do when you're in a disempowered state, the best thing to do is to take just a few minutes to write a list of your accomplishments – things you know you did really well, things you are proud of yourself for, times that you excelled or handled something really well. Ten is a good number to start with. Twenty is even better. You may start out slow, but then it will kick in. Remember that time you . . . ? Yeah, that. Write it down. Think back over challenges you have faced and overcome. Something you got done against the odds or against a time constraint. What kindness have you extended to another? Times you've gone out of your way to do something or do it right. Multi-faceted projects you've completed. The question is, What accomplishments, both large and small, can you acknowledge?

Once you've listed your accomplishments, note the strengths, skills, qualities, knowledge, or resources that created your success. **We tend to dissect our failures in order to understand what went wrong, but we seldom take the time to look at our successes to acknowledge or understand what went right and how we created the successful outcome.** We also tend to overlook or diminish our own strengths and abilities, so it can be helpful to ask for input from someone you can trust to give you honest, POSITIVE perspective on your qualities.

What you learn from doing this exercise will 1) remind you of all the gifts, skills and talents you do possess, 2) remind you how amazing you are, and 3) give you the clarity and confidence to create success from your present challenges.

If you do the "It's Too Much" exercise from the previous section and you break down the things that are overwhelming into smaller tasks, that will also help you see – especially at the level of the chunked, specific tasks – that you are capable and competent and equal to anything on your list.

Give yourself the gift of admiring and acknowledging your list of past successes and the skills you have. Remind yourself that *of course* you are enough and *of course* you can handle whatever was overwhelming you. It's not selfish or prideful to honestly value your greatest strengths and qualities. This is how you deliver your greatest value in the world, and this is what helps you feel most fulfilled.

And, if you are really actually lacking something in this situation -- literally do not have the skill or knowledge required -- that doesn't mean you're not enough, but it does mean you need some assistance. So, stop and take the time to find or remind yourself of the resources available to assist you (see the "There's Not Enough" section above. Maybe Violet is a great proofreader and she can help. Or Collin knows exactly how to embed a video in a PowerPoint. Perhaps your sister would be happy to listen to your presentation and give you a few tips for making it more engaging or shorter or whatever.

In short, counteract "I'm Not Enough" with all the ways you are. And if you have actual shortcomings in one or two areas, ask for some help. The worst thing you can do is get self-critical, judge yourself as lacking and start to call yourself names. If you're in that pattern, (*I'm an idiot, I'm so disorganized, I'm lousy at this*) then jump right to the Language section in Chapter 6 to interrupt that pattern as quickly as possible.

Summary: The purpose of this chapter was to provide tools for counteracting the Limiting Beliefs that are creating and contributing to your overwhelm. When you become aware of the limiting beliefs of I'm Going to Die, It's All Too Much, There's Not Enough, and I'm Not Enough, you can catch and shift your reaction. The other main contributor to your sense of being overwhelmed in your life is your pattern of Language, Attention and Belief, which I'll teach you how to overcome in the next chapter.

Chapter 6

OVERCOMING OVERWHELM: RE-PATTERNING LANGUAGE, ATTENTION & BEHAVIOR

"Your life is the sum result of all the choices you make, both consciously and unconsciously. If you can control the process of choosing, you can take control of all aspects of your life. You can find the freedom that comes from being in charge of yourself."
~ Robert F. Bennett, lawyer and politician

How To Overcome Your LAB Pattern

Your unique pattern of **L**anguage, **A**ttention and **B**ehavior (LAB) is the active mechanism by which you create and sustain your Limiting Beliefs and your experience of feeling overwhelmed. I am happy to report that even subtle shifts in any of these elements can interrupt or stop your pattern of overwhelm.

LANGUAGE

Language is perhaps the most powerful of the mechanisms that create and sustain our pattern of overwhelm. Each of us is impacted by what we say to ourselves as well as how we say it. Disempowering language that contributes to overwhelm shows up in a number of ways including:

- The Bully Voice
- Absolutes
- Shoulds

The Bully Voice

Many of us say things to ourselves we would NEVER say to anyone else, even our worst enemy. You may be in the habit of calling yourself names such as *loser, idiot, moron, slob* or . . . fill in the blank. That negative internal dialogue is feeding your overwhelm and *disempowering* rather than empowering you to do anything different or handle what is in front of you. Calling yourself names is not the least bit helpful. In fact, it's absolutely destructive.

Imagine watching a child trying to ride a bike and people yelling out, "You're so uncoordinated, you're so dumb, you'll never get this." You'd be appalled, as would anyone watching. And imagine the internal state it's creating in the child. Is it helpful in any way? Or does it just ensure failure?

To change the habit of this destructive way you talk to yourself, you must simply decide to **ban the bully**. We all have a version of that voice – it's just that some people choose not to listen to it. They ignore it; and just like with the school bully, if you don't provide the food of your attention and the satisfaction of a charged reaction, then it will lessen in frequency and intensity.

If you think your bully is helping you somehow, consider this. I ask my clients if that voice makes them feel more confident or less. The answer is always, "less." I then ask if the bully makes them more likely to take action or less. The answer, again, is always, "less." So if listening to the voice makes you less confident and less likely to take action, why would you want to listen to it?

My client Jeremy had an important moment of recognition when he realized that the voice of his bully *was not him*, and more important, that *he didn't have to listen to it anymore.* In a visualization, Jeremy imagined drop-kicking that bully through football goalposts. He celebrated as if he had just scored 3 points for his team. Each time that voice came up, instead of listening to it, Jeremy interrupted the pattern to score another 3 points.

You can actually decide to use encouraging and supportive language with yourself instead of critical, belittling or disempowering language. This may sound simplistic and maybe even a bit silly or childish, but it's not. Language is very powerful; and using different language is both helpful and kind. *And it actually makes a difference.*

Rather than speaking unkind, unhelpful and critical words to yourself, be supportive, as you would wish another to be toward you. Encourage, rather than discourage yourself. Recognize and reinforce your strengths. Know that you're making the best choice you can under the circumstances. For example, you may criticize yourself as *lazy* and a *loser* or *unhealthy* or *irresponsible* for taking the kids through the fast food drive-thru again this week, even when you know it would be healthier to make fresh food at home. Instead, what about recognizing that you're doing the best you can? Notice that instead of dragging the kids through the supermarket and stressing yourself with preparing, serving and then cleaning up from dinner, you're choosing an alternative that will allow you to spend some quality time with them when you get home. Sometimes the choices we criticize ourselves for are actually in alignment with our values, and what we feel is most important in the moment.

Decide what kind of supportive messages you wish someone would give you, then give them to yourself. I know it may seem weird and uncomfortable, and maybe even childish to think about doing this. But I am asking you to try it . . . and just notice what the results are. My clients who learn to do this for themselves are always astounded by the difference it makes.

Ellen, a mother of three small children called herself names for losing patience when the kids were behaving like ... well... kids. To shift this unhelpful pattern (that only made her feel worse and also that she was hopeless as a mother) she instead reminded herself that every day she was learning and getting better at being a mom, and that she aspired to be guided by patience, caring, and love for her kids. When she talked to herself with this language instead, it became easier to be the mother she wanted to be. See how – and if – your "overwhelm" shifts in the face of supportive rather than critical language. You might be surprised.

Exercise: A simple way to begin to experiment with shifting language patterns is to find three positive adjectives to replace the less-than-positive names you regularly call yourself, and practice using them for a couple of weeks. Or you can choose just two or three qualities you wish you were demonstrating more often. Even if you're rolling your eyes at this positive self-talk suggestion, try it for yourself and see what happens. See if you actually feel different. You might be surprised at the power of language in your internal dialog.

Absolutes

It is common for absolutes like "always" and "never" to show up in people's language when they're in a state of overwhelm. Use this chart to help build your awareness of this unhelpful (and almost always inaccurate) language pattern. You can download a copy of this chart from the End Overwhelm Now website (www.EndOverwhelmNow.com) so that you can post it where it can best remind you to catch yourself using these words that can trigger or contribute to overwhelm:

Absolutes

Always	Never	Must/Have To	Perfectly
All	Only	Can't	Fail
Every	None	Not	Nobody

These words allow no room to move; they have no fluidity, no flexibility; they make no exception. They make you either 100% correct or 100% wrong. It's a pass/fail system with the odds stacked against you. When your brain hears these words, it recognizes the no-win situation, and responds accordingly.

Tracy, a highly successful salesperson, demonstrates a classic case of absolute language. She tells me, "I can never get a handle on all I have to do. I have more work than anyone and none of my colleagues helps out, so it all falls on me. Every time I think about how I can't catch up, it makes me crazy." Who wouldn't be overwhelmed with that story? There's no way out and no help in sight.

Exercise: Replace absolutes with words more representative of your real situation. For example, the reality is that Tracy *does* take action on her key action steps, and her colleagues *do* support her. Here's how Tracy reframed her language: "It's important to get a handle on my highest priorities, and I'm generally able to do that. And it's also important to ask my colleagues to help out when I'm running behind. My workload isn't that different from anyone else's and when I stay focused on what matters most, I can usually keep up." When she shifted her self-talk this way, she actually started to feel different and to experience her work situation in a different way. She found it uncanny how something this simple made a difference. But it did. And it does.

Familiarize yourself with the healthy, calming and truer alternatives to the absolutes and begin to practice them in your speech. Replace absolutes with words like:

Alternatives

Enough	Sometimes	Get To	Improve
Some	Possible	Can	Choose
Focus	Options	Opportunity	Better
Progress			

Shoulds

Overwhelm is often characterized by "shoulds," especially the vague, unmeasurable shoulds: "I *should* do more." "My boss *should* understand my workload." Or, here's a helpful one: "I *shouldn't* feel this way." "Shoulds" feed into overwhelm by creating an expectation of performance that you (or those around you) are unlikely to fulfill.

When you use "should" in regard to someone else, you're seeking to apply your rules to someone else's behavior. Since you can't force that person to conform to your rules, that "should" is wasted focus and wasted energy. When you use "should" for yourself, it usually means you don't have the energy or real desire to take the action you're "shoulding" about, but you have some sort of obligation or rule that won't let you off the hook. So you're in an energetic push-pull stalemate.

Begin noticing each time you use the word "should" in relation to tasks or actions. How often do you take action – really – in response to your "should" thoughts? Most people don't follow through on a "should" until they make it a "want" or a "must." And we often stack one "should" after another on ourselves. "I should call my mother-in-law, and I should exercise, and I should eat better, and I really should get that project done at work." Telling yourself you "should" do something is generally the equivalent of setting yourself up to fail.

Exercise: Stop "shoulding" on yourself. Whenever you catch yourself "should-ing," stop and make a decision. As Yoda in *Star Wars* so astutely said, "Do, or do not." Either make that action a priority and set a clear plan for when you'll do it, or let it go in some way, like putting it on a "do later" list that you periodically review. But keeping it in the forefront of your mind and torturing yourself with what you should be doing when it is actually not a priority, is a counterproductive energy drain. When ending overwhelm, it's important to set yourself up to win with the decisions you make.

The Lousy Question

Another key language pattern that contributes to overwhelm is the "Lousy Question." A lousy question assumes the worst case, puts the focus on the problem rather than a solution, and usually has no real or useful answer. Questions like, "What's wrong with me?" or, "Why am I so stuck?" or, "Will I ever get out of this mess?" qualify as lousy questions. To make matters worse, combine "should" and absolutes with a lousy question to create what I call doubt-inducing questions: "*Should* I look for a new job?" "What's the *best* thing to do?" "What if I don't do this *perfectly*?" These questions confuse your brain. It doesn't know how to evaluate "should," "best," or "perfectly," so it just loops or dead-ends. And when you can't answer the questions you're asking yourself, your brain believes it failed again.

Exercise: Replace lousy questions with powerful ones. Powerful questions include three elements:

1) They ask "what" or "how" instead of "why" or "why not,"

2) They are focused on the solution or what you want, not on the problem or what you *don't* want, and

3) They have a built-in supposition of success.

When you hear yourself ask a lousy question, stop and reframe it in a more supportive way. For example, a lousy question might be, "Why am I always passed over for promotion?" The word "why" causes your brain to go looking for an answer in the wrong direction. You're looking for an answer for why you are NOT promoted – and not just sometimes but *always* (which tells your brain in a subtle way that there's no hope). When you're focused on why you are never promoted, you aren't problem-solving to *get* promoted. A better version of that question would be, "How can I make it even easier to get the job promotion I want?" Or "What can I do that will help me get promoted?" Take a few minutes to find some examples of lousy questions that you ask yourself, and see if you can reframe them. It actually shifts your brain into a resourceful focus, and is a great way to counteract feelings of overwhelm and powerlessness.

Eavesdrop On Yourself

One of the most important ways to stay out of overwhelm is to be aware of the patterns of language you're using. Eavesdrop on your internal conversation. Notice when you use one of the language patterns above, or any language that makes you feel overwhelmed. Your language may be stacking all you have to do, so you feel "it's all too much." Your language may be lamenting that you "never" have what you need (the trigger of "there's not enough"). Or your bully voice may be making you feel that "you're not enough." Motivational speaker Jim Rohn advised, ***"Every day, stand guard at the door of your mind."*** Recognize the powerful impact that language has on how you feel about yourself and your situation. If you have trouble watching for yourself, ask those who spend time with you to notice what types of disempowering language you habitually use.

Think of your language like a radio station. If you're not paying attention, anything can be playing in the background. As soon as you notice that you don't like what's playing, you can change the station on the radio, from upsetting news to soothing music. Likewise, you can change the language in your head from self-deprecating junk to empowering messages. You get to choose.

ATTENTION

Language and attention often work together to create or increase overwhelm, but attention also stands on its own as a powerful overwhelm dynamic.

We've seen attention at work when a little kid in a store is having a tantrum over a toy he wants -- must have -- NOW. There might be a hundred or a thousand other items in the store, but this one thing has caught his attention and he's become fixated on it . . . unless and until his parents are able to distract him and/or direct his attention elsewhere. When we're in overwhelm, our attention is like the child's, it becomes fixated on certain things and we lose sight of others.

Attention, quite simply, is the mechanism through which you intentionally or unintentionally direct your focus.

The metaphor I like to use for attention is taking a photograph. The scene may include a garden, house, bird, flowers, buildings, a person, wires, ground, sky, etc. When you are taking a picture, you choose what you want as the focal point of the photograph. You can make it a close-up or take in the whole landscape. You can decide to have the person or building or bird in the shot or not. You can make it clear and crisp, or blur the focus to change the feeling. By changing focus, light, angle and subject you determine the look and feel of the photograph: bright or dark, somber or uplifting, serious or light-hearted. In a beautiful garden, there might be one small piece of trash that has blown in from the curb. You could focus on that and make the whole photograph just about that, or widen the focus to the whole garden and the small piece of trash wouldn't even be noticeable. What you focus on, and how you focus the shot, is what the story of the photograph becomes.

Similarly, where you direct your attention, and how you focus it, determines the look and feel of your situation, the story of your situation, or of your life.

When it comes to overwhelm, what you focus on creates and sustains the state you've put yourself in. When, for example, the

"It's too much" trigger is at play, your mind tends to go in circles over and over on your enormous to-do list. ("I have to do __, and I have to do __, and then there's __," and on and on). Speed up those thoughts to a frenetic pace, and you've got a good case of overwhelm. Learning to shift focus is one of the most effective ways of dissipating this crazy-making pattern and restoring yourself to sanity.

Learning to re-direct your attention is a critical aspect of overcoming overwhelm because **overwhelm has the effect of making you focus on the negative** . . . how much there is to do, what isn't getting done, what you're doing wrong, what you lack. **It also focuses your attention on what you fear most**, even if you don't know what that is, rather than on what *matters* most. These are the automatic or default positions of attention when you're overwhelmed. To overcome overwhelm, you have to learn to shift your pattern of attention.

Attention and Emotion

Researchers estimate that we have about 60,000 thoughts per day. When you let your mind fixate on thoughts of everything you have to do that isn't getting done, what happens? Or focus on the thought that there isn't enough, or you'll never get ahead? How you're not following through in the way you should? On what's *not* working? Those kinds of thoughts trigger a very different experience than choosing to focus on your progress, what's going right, the resources you have at hand, etc.

Almost every thought you have is wired into your nervous system with a positive or negative association or charge. In 1975, the movie *Jaws* about a predatory shark terrified audiences around the world. It was the highest grossing movie of its time I think, in part, because it riveted the attention (sitting in the dark watching a 30 foot screen is helpful for that) and engendered such intense emotion

For weeks after watching the movie, I was nervous any time I was around water, even getting into the bathtub, though of course there was no risk of sharks there, or really anywhere for me. And like most people, just the first few notes of the music signaling the approach of the shark set me on edge, though again there was no danger of sharks.

When we have an intense emotional reaction by focusing our attention on what is causing us concern – for example a long to-do list, or a big project or a presentation or a test or whatever – we are working with a similar principle. We create a similar stimulus-response reaction every time we look at the to-do list or think about the presentation and feel overwhelmed, even if we weren't overwhelmed a moment before. Just as we can learn to associate fear with a certain song, we can inadvertently train ourselves to associate overwhelm with our to-do list.

A client recently told me that it didn't make sense that she got so very anxious when looking at her to-do list. But because it had become a conditioned response for her, every time she thought about what she had to do, she had the same response. This kind of intense emotional response is not only unpleasant, it also engenders avoidance behavior, which is one of the least helpful reactions when we're overwhelmed with things we need to do.
Recognize how the focus that creates our Jaws-like anxiety paralyzes us more than empowers us. We CAN shift our attention to interrupt this pattern. The benefit: our to-do list becomes a tool

we use, rather than one that uses us; and that project that's due can become just a project again, instead of a self-perpetuating cycle of anxiety and overwhelm.

You will discover that the more you focus on "all there is to do" and how little you feel capable of doing it because there's not enough time or know-how or help or whatever – the pattern we call "stacking and lacking" – the more negative emotion you will feel and the more overwhelm you will create.

Conversely, focus on your strengths, remember the resources at your disposal, and remind yourself of your successes. This is how you can consciously create positive, resourceful and empowering emotions, which will shift your pattern of overwhelm.

The more you practice either positive or negative patterns of thought, the more habitual they will become. Notice what it feels like to scare yourself with "stacking" thoughts versus feeling confident that you can handle it. Learn to direct your attention to how you *can* manage what is in front of you, and overwhelm begins to dissipate. You may still have a lot to do, but you won't be drowning in the emotions of overwhelm.

Default Mode

Our brains tend to operate in well-worn patterns. We are generally thinking the same thoughts we've always thought in response to what's happening in the outside world. We do this because it's easy; our brains are most efficient when processing habitual patterns of thought. And we do this because our habitual thoughts actually get *programmed* as the default route in our brains. The movie *What The Bleep Do We Know!?* does a great job of explaining synaptic activity in our brains and how – just like you probably take the same route to work every morning -- our thoughts literally take the routes they know best. Neural pathways are a real thing. Even if you don't like where your brain's habitual patterns take you, it's where your thoughts are going to go without conscious intervention.

Gaining control of your overwhelm – indeed getting better control of your life --requires that you *consciously override* your brain's default processing. Luckily, you *can* train your brain and your thoughts to go in a different direction simply by – like a camera lens -- shifting focus. Thanks to brain plasticity we can change our neural pathways and make new and lasting changes in how we process our world and our experience.

The Art of Directing Attention

The way to override the negative (default) focus when you're overwhelmed is through intentional practice. In the same way that how we focus the camera lens determines the composition of a photo, redirecting your attention creates a different view of your situation.

How do you learn to redirect your attention?

1) You understand that you have the power to choose, and that *you* get to decide what to focus on.

2) You make the intention to shift from stacking and lacking thoughts to consciously directing your attention toward desired outcomes, possibilities, and what you want.

3) You practice consciously directing your attention in different situations and in different ways (and, by the way, create new neural pathways as you do).

Here are some ways to practice intentional focus:

- **Catching Habitual Thoughts** - When we do something repetitious or mundane – things that don't require our conscious attention because we've got them on auto-pilot – our mind is free to visit its habitual places. The next time you do something routine, like driving to the grocery store or vacuuming, see if you can catch where your attention goes without conscious direction. The purpose of this exercise is to notice how often you default to the thinking that creates your overwhelm. See if you can catch the ongoing chatter in your mind about how much you have to do, or what's wrong or what you fear or what you're not doing that you need to be doing or what someone else should be doing. How many of your thoughts are on what you have accomplished or constructive planning or about things you actually have some control over?

  As you can catch these thoughts, you can *redirect them*. Using the power of your attention, ***decide to focus on other things***, on constructive thoughts (see the Beliefs section above) that will empower you rather than disempower you by feeding your overwhelm. Is it that simple? Yes. You get to be in the driver's seat of where your attention goes. When I challenge my clients to do this exercise, they are always surprised at what their minds habitually do. As an example, my client Bev exclaimed one day, "I consider myself a positive person, but I realize I have a lot of negative, judgmental thoughts." With this realization, Bev more readily catches herself and makes the shift.

Another way to catch habitual thoughts is to set a periodic alarm on your phone or watch, and jot down what you are thinking about each time the alarm goes off. Also, because thoughts engender feelings, take a moment to note how you were feeling as you were focused on those thoughts. It takes just a few seconds to check in with your thoughts and feelings, and you'll be surprised at what you learn about your brain when you take a snapshot of what was going on in the moment.

- **Counting the Green Lights** - Humans are programmed to notice what's wrong; it's a hard-wired survival mechanism. Nothing was gained for our ancestors by noticing a beautiful tree or the song of a bird, or how well everything seemed to be going... but a heck of a lot was gained – their very lives – if they noticed a strange rustling in the bush or a far-off growl or worried about storing enough food for the coming winter. With survival our highest priority, our brains look for what's wrong, not what's right. But that ancient programming, while still very much in play, no longer serves us. Unfortunately, evolution takes a while to catch up to environment, so our brains are still working on the original factory-installed software. However, by consciously directing our own attention, we can override this tendency -- and have much more happy, relaxed and functional lives as a result.

Here's an interesting exercise a yoga teacher suggested to a friend. You may want to try your own version. The teacher recommended my friend put a roll of pennies in his right pocket and move one penny to his left pocket every time something "good" or "positive" or pleasant happened in his day. The goal was to move as many pennies as possible. Things started slowly, but once he got the hang of it, the pace of penny transfer increased. First he started to notice every green light he hit, when normally he would only note with exasperation when the lights were red. Next he moved a penny for *not* having to wait in line at the bank. Another penny moved for the liquor store having his brand of single malt scotch in stock; not a big deal, but it sure would have caught his attention if they'd been out. He started to have fun with the game, moving a penny for the copier having plenty of paper and toner when he had to make a quick copy, for not having to wait on hold at Best Buy, for a calm family dinner, for the cable working just fine. This silly little game helped him realize that he seldom noticed what was going right, not because he was an especially negative person (he wasn't). It's just that's where our attention naturally goes, especially when we're in overwhelm. Now, whenever he feels tension building, he starts to count the green lights -- and everything else that's going right -- and it restores his brain to a healthier pattern of attention.

- **Watching Your Yesses** - One of the things that gets people into overwhelm is saying "Yes" as a reflexive response. *Yes* because they're afraid to say *no*, *yes* because *no* might disappoint someone, *yes* because they should, *yes* because their boss or co-worker will give them a bad report, *yes* because they want to be liked or thought well of, *yes* because they're caretakers, or want to be superman or superwoman. The next time someone asks you to do something, notice where your mind goes. Is your first thought that of course you have to say yes? Or the instant panic of how will you ever get it done (pre-supposing you have to get it done before you have even agreed)? Catch your habitual response by paying attention next time a request is made. You may be able to wait before responding. Take a minute to think about your existing priorities and realistically assess your availability. Check in with how you actually feel about the request: is it something you *want* to do? Or *can* do? Have time for? Have interest in? Is it your responsibility or someone else's? The purpose of this presence exercise is to override the default, knee-jerk reaction of where your attention automatically goes. Instead, bring your attention to *how* you will get it done, or whether it is appropriate to even say yes. Catching this pattern of response and interrupting the pattern is a task of attention.

- **Watching Your Words** - One of the most powerful tools for redirecting attention is language. If you feel you're going to die if it doesn't all get done, or John is going to kill you, or you can't handle it, etc., language can often save you because language directs and reinforces attention. Try saying to yourself, "Of course I'm not going to die; I'm going to be fine" or "John may not be thrilled but he is certainly not going to kill me, he may even understand," or "I'm not loving this, but I certainly can handle it. And I've handled similar things dozens of times before," directs your attention from dire consequences to reasonable assessment. We have a whole Language section up above, so if you skipped over it, now might be a good time to go back and read it. Language is a game changer.

Attention and Organization

Your brain needs to recognize patterns or it becomes anxious. An example you may have experienced is listening to a band or an orchestra warm up before a performance. As each musician tests their instrument individually, the cacophony of sounds is unpleasant and uncomfortable because your brain can't find the pattern of notes. You may even find it's hard to concentrate on anything else while your brain is subjected to that lack of order. However, as soon as the orchestra begins playing together and your brain recognizes a pattern (music), there's an instant relaxation.

This is also your brain's reaction with overwhelm. When you're feeling overwhelmed, you must give the brain an environment of order and organization to calm the mind, relax the tension and send the message that the situation is manageable. With order restored, your higher-order functions like decision making and problem solving will be more accessible. You may need to create order internally (organizing what's going on inside your head), externally (organizing what's around you), or both.

Reducing Internal Chaos – Organizing Your Thoughts

Throughout this book I've pointed out how it's your thinking that is the *real* source of overwhelm. There are many things that can *trigger* overwhelm, but the experience of overwhelm must include a pattern of thought. And the single best way that I know to end overwhelm is to be able to organize your thinking: organizing your thoughts from the random frenetic chaos of overwhelm into a manageable order. We do this by *directing attention in very specific ways.* This reduces the mental and emotional churn of overwhelm; it also leads to sensible rather than random, frenetic or nonproductive action.

Looking at what you think is overwhelming you, here are 4 steps to directing your attention in service of organizing your thinking. These are best done in writing. The act of simply embodying your swirling thoughts by writing them down and making them "real" can reduce overwhelm.

1) **WHAT?** When in the throes of overwhelm, people tend to focus on specific tasks, and can easily lose sight of the actual outcome they're after. "Oh my God, I have to get that paper written by Friday and I have to study for that final" is task-oriented thinking. What are you really after? Learning the material? Finishing the semester in good standing? Graduating? Becoming a teacher? Becoming a good teacher? What's the real result you're after? Ask yourself *what is the important outcome here?* When we're overwhelmed, we tend to get mired in the problem rather than focusing on the outcome. Clearly state what you want to accomplish, and how you'll know when you've gotten there. Get specific. Give your brain a positive outcome – a clear "what" to focus on and work toward, rather than letting it swim in the chaos of the many tasks at hand. You may have one or two big outcomes, or you may have important outcomes in the major areas of your life. For example, you may have dozens (or hundreds) of things to do for work, but what is **really most important**? Your overwhelmed brain may *think* it's all important, but if you could only focus on a few key things (which, of course, is all you can do anyway), what would those few things be?

It takes some practice to keep your focus on the "what." However, the more you do it, the more you will train your brain to create this focus. Simply asking yourself, "what matters MOST in this situation?" "If I can get only one thing done, what one thing would feel the best to complete/accomplish?" Or, for an area of life that may be overwhelming to you, "What do I most want?" Give yourself permission to be clear about what you want, even if the answer is scary or complicated. That clarity of focus will be reinforced by our subsequent steps.

To give you a very simple example, I recently stopped by a friend's house as she was cleaning out her hall closet. When I arrived she was surrounded by what could have been overwhelming piles of disorganized stuff. But she wasn't freaking out or the least bit overwhelmed. Even if the stuff was disorganized, her *thinking* was organized. She never lost sight of her outcome. Her attention wasn't distracted by the piles of boots and gloves and mittens and snow melt and umbrellas and backpacks and what-all because her attention was on the big-picture "what:" *cleaning out and organizing the closet.* As long as you keep the "what" clearly in mind, you can stay clear and focused on the task at hand. Defining and staying focused on your desired outcome is an important intervention whenever overwhelm threatens.

2) **WHY?** Knowing the *why* of your outcome also helps focus and organize your brain in the right direction. What is it you want to gain by taking these actions, or undertaking this project? How will you feel upon completion? The more compelling your "why" is, the more excitement and energy you'll have to follow through. Even if it's a mundane task you've been avoiding, think about how good it will feel to get it off your list and done. Sometimes your "why" will help to clarify your "what." For example, I write down that my big reason to clean out the basement is to give my kids a fun place to play and invite their friends over. As I think about that, I realize that the rest of the house will be quieter as a result. And

that helps me realize how much I want a quieter environment. Now I'm clearer about what I want, and have even more reasons to organize the basement.

3) **HOW?** What are a few simple ways to start achieving the outcome you want now? How can you organize the steps to make it easy to follow through? Who can help you make it easier, faster, or more successful? What do you need to let go of (stuff, old beliefs, pleasing other people, etc.) to have the outcome you want? Let your brain look at a few simple steps for beginning so that it understands that there *is* an orderly process that can get to the outcome. Your brain will start to relax and you will be able to see your way clear.

4) **WHEN?** How urgent is this really? Take a minute and answer that question. What other parts of your mind, and your life, are being impacted by this situation or because of your overwhelm around it? And when you have your answer, figure out when you can devote the time to start on it, to make substantive progress or to complete it. Make a time, whether it's now or a specific time later, so your attention doesn't keep running in circles around it. Once your mind knows specifically when that activity will be addressed, it can relax. If it has no idea when, or if, you're going to address that overwhelm trigger, your brain will keep churning the same concerns, worries, questions, and anxiety.

These four questions, which we revisit in the Behavior section, can help organize your thinking around and calm your sense of overwhelm.

Doreen started her home-based business using the same desk she used for bills, the kids' school papers, photos, mail and the piles of papers and stuff that a family of five accumulates. She also had stacks of printed material for her new business: training manuals, marketing materials and new client paperwork. Although she was excited about the business, she dreaded "going to work." Just walking into that room triggered the feeling of overwhelm, followed by the disempowering sense of "I don't know where to begin" every time she looked at the piles on her desk. No wonder her days weren't particularly productive; her brain literally couldn't function properly in the face of the "mess." Not to mention the disempowering self-talk of "I'm so disorganized, how can I effectively run a business?" and the resulting feeling of being out of control.

Before Doreen -- or any of us -- can functional productively, we must have a generally organized environment, internally and externally. The orchestra has to be playing some semblance of music; we don't function well in the face of disordered, disturbing cacophony. Doreen used the What-Why-How-When model to organize her thinking.

Her outcome (the "What") was to organize the desk so that she could efficiently run her business and manage the family's papers as well. Doreen was very clear about her "Why:" initially, being organized would get her out of the delay and procrastination she was experiencing, and she also wanted to be free of her disempowering self-talk. As we got deeper into what she really wanted and why, ultimately she realized that being successful in her business would bring in additional money, would give her a sense of pride and satisfaction, and would help her clients with the solutions they needed to be happier and more successful. These were great motivators for her.

We tackled the "How" by bringing focus through a series of questions, and taking small, specific actions. Doreen needed to categorize the paperwork and materials so she knew where to find what she needed. But the thought of going through *every single thing* threw her back into overwhelm. So she did just one simple step. She got a box for each category of activity (there were only about seven, although it *seemed* like more) and quickly put everything in its category box. She kept her attention *just* on the sorting process, not in making any decisions about the items themselves. In just a couple of hours, Doreen cleared the desk and had seven categories that allowed her brain to organize everything that came through the office. She then created a plan of When, and in what order, to tackle organizing each of the category boxes. One category at a time was a manageable chunk for Doreen to handle. And best of all, she was excited to walk in, sit down to an organized desk, and work on her business.

External Chaos – Organizing What's Around You

Doreen's not alone in needing an organized space to have an organized mind. Few of us can effectively focus and work in a cluttered environment. A colleague in my consulting days was known for having an office that looked like a bomb had gone off. Somehow his powers of focus were so great that he could work in the total chaos. However, I've always wondered how much *more* effective he might have been by spending a few minutes each day to create some order. I've also worked with people who were so busy keeping their environments "just so," that it limited their productivity. Only you can choose what's right for you; extensive research of attention has shown, though, that we are easily distracted, and after being distracted, require several seconds to reconnect with the task. So your environment may be having a greater impact on your overwhelm than you realize.

Notice if your physical environment is a trigger for your overwhelm. If so, take just a few minutes to determine what few things you could do to feel a greater sense of order. Doreen, for example, needed a clean workspace in order to concentrate. Jenny, an author who worked from home, had to have the kitchen cleaned up to do her best work.

If you need additional support in this arena, there are many approaches to the concept of organizing to prevent or minimize overwhelm. Greg McKeown, in his book *Essentialism: The Disciplined Pursuit of Less* talks about distinguishing the "vital few" important things from the "trivial many." The Minimalists (www.theminimalists.com) have become popular by challenging us to dramatically reduce the number of possessions in exchange for greater simplicity and life satisfaction. The massive success of *The Life-Changing Magic of Tidying-Up* (over 2 million copies sold in a little over a year since publication) is evidence that many of us are looking for the solution to organizing our stuff, and, ultimately, our lives. Each of these resources is a reminder that organizing our environments can help organize our thinking, and help us end overwhelm.

Remember that your environment also includes digital and communication devices. The rings and pings of phone, email and social media can distract your focus, and contribute to overwhelm through a fear of missing out. Trust me, you won't die if you miss out on a social media post. Your brain will work so much better when you give it a "clean" digital environment.

The Field of Our Focus

Another important aspect of focusing our attention (rather than letting it focus us) is beautifully laid out in Steven Covey's classic book, *The Seven Habits of Highly Effective People*. In the book, Covey makes a distinction between the "Circle of Concern" and the "Circle of Influence." The Circle of Concern encompasses things that we might worry about, but over which we have *no* control. The Circle of Influence encompasses those things over which we have *some* control. Covey's admonition is to **focus on the Circle of Influence** and not the Circle of Concern.

People are often overwhelmed because they're focusing on the things they can't control. Since your brain is always trying to keep up with its environment, when you focus on what you can't control, *of course* your brain goes into overwhelm. That's why it can be so overwhelming to watch the news. It's all bad news, and there's nothing you can do about it.

Use this series of questions to help you refocus from the Circle of Concern to your Circle of Influence when you find yourself feeling overwhelmed:

1) **Can I do anything about this now?** If so, take some action, no matter how small. Make a phone call, schedule an appointment on your calendar, anything to send the message to your brain that you have control over what needs to be done. You are therefore empowered rather than in the non-resourceful state of powerlessness.

2) **If I can't do anything about this now, can I do something about it later? And when?** Let's say it's midnight on a Saturday,

and you need to call a business that's not open on the weekend. The answer would be "Yes, I can do something about it, but not until Monday morning." Set a calendar appointment or phone reminder or put a post-it note on your desk -- do something to set yourself up to take action on Monday and *put it out of your mind for now.*

3.) ***If I can't do anything about this now or later, can I do anything about this at all?*** If not, is it worth my peace of mind? If it's not worth my peace of mind, how can I let it go? And if I can't let it go, when can I schedule a time in the future to worry about it? Set an appointment with yourself for a future time to worry and be overwhelmed. Put it in your calendar or planner just like you would a doctor's appointment. If your brain knows there's a placeholder to worry about it, you can keep reminding yourself of your appointment to focus on that particular concern. In the meantime, what else could you focus on that would help you feel more in control and successful?

My client Mona felt compelled to watch the news. But random violence, such as terrorist attacks, triggered Mona's fear and she became overwhelmed with the worry that she or someone she loved would be impacted. Obviously there was no specific way Mona could prevent random things from happening. We looked at how the overwhelm and anxiety were impacting her. Rather than taking care of her family in a loving, caring way, she was anxious. So we first looked for ways to get news that didn't trigger her as much, and then she chose to set aside a specific time when she would allow herself to worry. When she did become anxious, she reminded herself she could worry on Sunday morning. By the time Sunday came around, she didn't want to spend her time being anxious and worried. She kept moving the appointment out until she realized that she really could choose not to pay attention to those things outside her control.

Pay Attention

The goal of this section was to give you a few simple, specific, concrete strategies to redirect your attention to diminish overwhelm. The first and most important step is to become aware of *how your attention is contributing to your overwhelm*. Because so much of how we direct our attention is habitual, simply catching ourselves and choosing to be intentional can be powerful. With **choice and practice**, and some of the exercises we've provided, *you truly can redirect your mind from overwhelm to a more empowering focus*.

Now, with an ordered environment, mind and thoughts, you can move into taking action . . . the Behavior portion of LAB.

BEHAVIOR

> *"Every time we act in the presence of our fear we dilute its power and we amplify our own. To fight fear, act. To increase fear – wait, put off, postpone."*
> ~ David Joseph Schwartz

The third factor in the LAB triad is your behavior – what you actually do or don't do. Behavior generally follows language and attention. You may find that redirecting your attention and changing your internal dialogue often produces different behavior. However, sometimes you have to take intentional action in the arena of behavior itself to end overwhelm. Behavior is generally not the driving force in *creating* overwhelm (beliefs, language and attention do that) but it is the driving force in *perpetuating* the cycle of overwhelm.

Overwhelm can cause even the most effective person to behave in ineffectual ways: failing to take action, taking the wrong action or taking half-hearted action. This creates a feedback loop that perpetuates the feeling of overwhelm, and amplifies the negative language and focus. Once we start consistently behaving in a certain way, we associate the behavior with who we are. It becomes part of our identity. Notice when you create labels for yourself: "I'm a procrastinator," or "I'm not good at following through," or even worse, "I'm just a screw-up." Instead of recognizing that a simple behavior needs to change, you may believe that you must change who you are. Changing your personality or your essential nature is much harder than changing a behavior.

There are two categories of changes we can make in the behavioral arena when we are facing or already in a state of overwhelm. One involves training ourselves to be in *intentional action* instead of fight, flight or freeze mode. Useful, appropriate, productive action creates a cycle that makes it that much easier to take action the next time you're feeling overwhelmed. The other has to do with behaviors that *take care of our physical bodies*.

Action Begets Action

Newton's First Law of Motion (The Law of Inertia) states that a body at rest tends to stay at rest, which is what we usually think of when we hear the word "inertia," but we forget the very critical second half of the law, which is that **a body in motion tends to stay in motion**.

An important principle of the End Overwhelm Now process is that taking action is critical for counteracting your pattern of overwhelm. Unfortunately, one of the things that happens when we're truly overwhelmed is that we can find it almost impossible to take action. It's part of the "freeze" response; we feel powerless and don't know where to begin.

Here is where the "Behavior" piece of LAB comes into play. Behavior may be the third leg of LAB, but without it, the process doesn't work. Just as a three-legged stool needs that third leg to stand – the LAB triad must include actual behavioral changes. Changing your language and focus help only so much. Then you have to DO something different.

Getting into the habit of taking action – even when you're overwhelmed – accomplishes a number of things, not the least of which is that once you're in motion, it becomes that much easier to stay in motion. Here are a few strategies to help with behaving your way out of overwhelm:

1) **Chunk and Celebrate It**: Although the actions of "chunking" tasks and celebrating accomplishments are two separate steps, I have them combined in one step for this reason: they work best together to counteract the paralysis of overwhelm.

We tend to procrastinate when a task is too big and/or too vague to take confident action. A frequent pattern is to delay what we need to be doing because it's hard or complex or we don't have enough time or "it's all too much." Even beginning seems impossible. We often build it up in our minds to be even bigger and harder than it is. Then when we finally do take action, we beat ourselves up anyway, feeling that it was too little too late, should have been done better, should have been done sooner, etc. This pattern of inaction and then judgment rather than reward *makes the brain want to avoid action in the future* because *it doesn't feel good.*

In contrast, consider the process of chunking and celebrating. What I mean by chunking is to break tasks down into manageable action steps. The goal is to give yourself the gift of following through with some actions, no matter how small, so you can experience a sense of accomplishment. For example, if you need to prepare a presentation or a paper, take 10 minutes to simply list the key points. While you're in the flow with that task, write down one or two next specific actions before you finish that task. Then smile and acknowledge yourself for taking that action. Your acknowledgement can be telling yourself, "good job," or cheering "whoo hoo!" or putting a big, fat checkmark next to that item on your list with satisfaction. This is why accountability to someone else tends to work so well; we're motivated to tell someone else, "I finished it," rather than, "I failed."

Taking small steps and then *celebrating* them teaches your brain that it is satisfying and rewarding to take action; that action *feels good.* As a result, your brain will want to take more action. You've now also started to associate the next tasks on the list with feeling good, because you thought of those right before celebrating. This approach seems small, and seems like it moves you only incrementally toward getting the thing DONE, but it actually works wonders. *And it is teaching your brain a new pattern.*

Marissa had avoided writing a pile of thank you notes from her 50th birthday. It wasn't the most important thing on her list, but it was eating at her in a way that had become an energy drain. She felt like a bad person for not acknowledging all that had been done to make her birthday special, yet she couldn't get started on the notes. We chunked it to start with the smallest step – just addressing the envelopes. Her task became simply to find the addresses and write them on the envelopes. That's it.

It sounded silly (chunking in the extreme) but it also sounded very do-able, so she did it. And once she did, she was suddenly in the space to start on the first note. And for some reason she could hardly explain to herself, she wrote all eight of them. Finished them that night. Maybe because that initial task was something she could so easily complete, maybe because doing something (anything) felt so good she just kept going, or maybe it's because of the very real principal that action begets action and a body in motion tends to stay in motion. "It turns out," she said to me, "that momentum is real – and that the expression about 'being on a roll' is a real thing, because once I got started, I just kept rolling along."

Yup.

It's an actual law of physics as we've already discussed. That's why taking ACTION – any action -- and feeling good about that action, is such a great way to counteract overwhelm.

2) **Plan It Out**: My clients who are the most committed to planning their days and weeks are the least likely to experience overwhelm. Maybe it's because their thinking is clearer, but I believe it's because the planning process -- even imperfectly done (and what is the "perfect" plan in a chaotic world, anyway?) – involves managing Attention, Language and Behavior, so the brain feels a sense of control. That sense of control helps us realize that we can, indeed, manage whatever we need to. That's not to say that if you're a good planner you'll never be overwhelmed again;

however, the process of thinking through priorities, intentionally creating a plan, and then having that as a guidepost for success will help you reduce the chaos that contributes to overwhelm.

3) **What – Why – How- When**: This four-question process from the Organizing Your Brain section can be helpful for planning action as well. Ask yourself:

- WHAT: What do you want to accomplish? *What is the most important outcome?* Be specific. When we're overwhelmed, we tend to focus on the problem, not what we ultimately want. Focusing on the desired outcome is a key to taking and maintaining action. Keep the end in mind. How will you know you are successful? Get as specific as you possibly can.

- WHY: Next, make sure you know *why* that is your desired outcome. What will you gain by achieving it? How will you feel? What will it mean if you *don't* work to get the outcome? Create some powerful excitement toward creating success. Even if it's a mundane task you've been avoiding, thinking about how good it will feel to get it off your list can help you be in action. You can even do the "5 Whys" process. Each time you answer the question, "Why do I want that outcome," ask again, "Why do I want *that* outcome?" Each time, seek to reveal an even deeper motivation behind your desire. This process will help you identify what really is most important about this situation, and may even guide you to an alternative – and possibly easier - way to get your desired outcome. For example, I want to finish that report to get my boss off my back. Why is it important to get my boss off my back? Because his nagging is annoying. Why is it important to end his nagging? I can't feel good about myself and my work when he's nagging. Why is that important? I really want to feel good about my work, and finishing the report is one way to feel good. Now that I've made a stronger link between finishing the report and how that will help me feel good about my work, I'm more motivated to complete it.

- HOW: What are a few simple ways to start achieving the outcome you want now? What are the steps and how can you organize the steps to make it easy to follow through? Who can help you make it easier, faster, or more successful? What do you need to intentionally take OFF of your list to have the outcome you want? Who do you need to talk to in order to set those expectations? What are your best first steps? What do you need to let go of (stuff, old beliefs, pleasing other people, etc.) to have the outcome you want? Often people are looking for the "right" or the "perfect" way to follow through. But that's virtually impossible. So give yourself permission to lay out the "how" the best you can at this moment, then begin following through and revise as you go along.

- WHEN: When can you devote some focused time to make substantive progress? Look at your calendar and decide when, specifically, you'll work on these key activities. Be realistic about the time it takes to complete the required tasks. A lot of people avoid planning because they're afraid they'll have to face the fact that they don't have time to do it all. But those who choose to end their pattern of being overwhelmed are committed to realistically looking at their commitments TODAY, rather than holding the unrealistic thought that they can somehow get it all done.

4) Start Anywhere and Be Willing to Start Before You're Ready.
The world is moving too fast, and you have too much to do, to think
that there will ever be a better time than NOW to get started on
whatever is on your plate that you keep avoiding. You'll never feel
more like doing it, you're not likely to have a major epiphany that
lays out the steps magically before you, and the world is not going
to stop until you're ready to take whatever step or steps you are
putting off before taking action.

My clients often tell me they're looking for the "right" or "best"
way to begin. Two quotations come to mind when I hear people
talking about this; one is Goethe's beautiful quote in which he
advises us to *"Begin it. Action has grace and magic and power in
it."* And indeed it does. The other, *"The gods send thread for the
web begun,"* is oft quoted but hard to find attribution for. And then
there's Nike's *Just Do It* which is a little less poetic than the other
two, but it still works.

Is there a "best" or "perfect" time to start? The only chance you'll ever
know the "best" way is in hindsight, after you've done it some other
way first. I often use the metaphor of walking along a wooded trail
where you can only see a few yards in front of you. As you progress
further down the path, the next segment of the path is revealed to
you. But you have to be in motion for that to happen. As you start
taking action on a big project, or begin organizing the things that
are overwhelming you, you'll learn more about the next steps to
take. Then the next. And soon you will get even better at taking that
kind of action. Your pattern of Language, Attention and Behavior
will begin reinforcing a more empowering course of action.

5)   **Get Support.** When you're overwhelmed, don't look for
someone to support you by commiserating with you – look for

someone to **support you in taking *action***. There's a critical difference – and one significantly more helpful and productive than the other. The more specific you are about what you need, the greater the likelihood that you'll find the right kind of support. It may just be someone to give you the push you need to take action; maybe it's someone to brainstorm possibilities and next steps; or maybe it's a mentor or advisor to guide you to the appropriate course of action. The most successful people I know have a strong network of people who they can call on as needed. Who is your network, and what other resources could empower you to take stronger, more effective action?

Use these five steps in whatever combination you need. They aren't sequential or dependent. They all will help you continue to take action, even when you're overwhelmed.

Taking Care Of Your Body

How you care for yourself physically affects your experience of overwhelm. Some physical influences that exacerbate overwhelm are:

- Lack of quality sleep

- Use of caffeine, sugar, or energy drinks to artificially raise your energy level

- Dehydration which slows your thought process

- Use of alcohol or drugs to escape or to slow yourself down

- Lack of movement (because movement naturally releases stress)

- Lack of natural sunlight and fresh air (because these elements help regulate your circadian rhythms)

Although in the Western world we tend to think of ourselves as minds that have bodies attached, the reality is that our physical nature is an integral part who we are and how we experience the world; and it has a significant impact on the functioning of our minds and emotions. When we're not taking care of our bodies (including artificially stimulating or suppressing our mental processes) we increase the risk of tripping ourselves into overwhelm or keeping ourselves there once we've arrived.

Even though I emphasize throughout this book that overwhelm is a mental problem -- a *thinking* problem -- I'm now going to tell you that part of ending your pattern and cycles of becoming overwhelmed is to pay attention to your body and take proper care. This means – even if you are overwhelmed with way too much to do and too little time to do it in -- it is important to:

- **Get enough sleep**, whatever that means for you. Even if you're on a deadline or overloaded with assignments and your tendency is to burn the midnight oil, *don't*. Please trust me on this. You will be significantly more resourceful, productive, effective, and efficient if you insist on getting your usual, or at least an adequate, amount of sleep.

- **Drink water** – Seems like a rather banal suggestion when you're feeling overwhelmed, but being dehydrated has been shown to actually slow down your thought processes. Think you don't have time to drink water and/or run to the bathroom every hour? Those 30 seconds will pay off big time. Drinking water is also grounding and calming, both excellent antidotes to overwhelm. I make my own "spa water" by putting thin slices of cucumber, lemon or orange into filtered water and letting it chill. There's a relaxing element to this combination; the spas are on to something.

- **Move** - Movement is a natural stress reliever. Lots of helpful chemicals get released into your system when you move your body, and movement also circulates blood and oxygen in a healthful, energizing way. When you feel the tension of overwhelm starting to build (*Oh my God, I'm never going to get this done in time*) get up and move around. If you don't have time for a workout, see if you can make time for a short walk, dance to a short song, or use an app or video to do a quick movement program. Our ancestors moved when they were stressed, and it still works for us today.

- **Monitor the use of artificial stimulants, relaxants and distractors** – Stimulants, like caffeine, can trigger the fight or flight response. Relaxants and distractors, such as alcohol and drugs, can induce the avoidance behavior that perpetuates the overwhelm cycle. These are ineffective ways to try to cope with overwhelm, but they can actually worsen the cycle.

- **Breathe** – The American Institute of Stress calls abdominal breathing the "super stress buster." The great thing about using breath to interrupt your triggers for overwhelm is that it's *always* available, and no special equipment is required.

Slow, deep, intentional breathing, in which you allow your belly and lungs to fully expand, triggers the relaxation response. Along with the breathing, you can also use the power of focus, as described in the Attention section above, to imagine yourself relaxed or empowered or confident or whatever emotional state will most support you right now.

These steps in shifting your Behavior pattern -- what you do and don't do when you're overwhelmed – will go a long way toward overcoming the ways your actions contribute to your overwhelm. When combined with the Language and Attention tools, you've got a surefire way of getting yourself out of overwhelm – and changing your patterns for good.

Playing Catch

In the two Overcoming Overwhelm chapters, we gave you the clues of how you create overwhelm through your Beliefs, Language, Attention and Behavior, as well as strategies and action steps to help you overcome your overwhelm.

By understanding how overwhelm happens in your mind and practicing what you can do to counteract it, you will begin to **experience yourself and your own shifts as the solution to your sense of overwhelm**. And soon you will be able to circumvent overwhelm altogether.

In the beginning of this re-patterning process, the first and most important thing you can do is to catch yourself.

Begin to notice your *Language*. See how often you can catch yourself in the not-enoughs, in the absolutes, in the lousy questions.

Practicing stopping a few times throughout your day to become aware of what you are focusing your *Attention* on: is it productive or disempowering? Are you noticing just the red lights or noticing the green ones as well?

Notice what happens if overwhelm is building and you change your *behavior* by taking *action* to support yourself through the exercises we provided. How do you feel if you remember to drink some water, breathe deeper, get up and move around? If you can follow just a few of the behavior suggestions and get yourself to take action on even the smallest step, what changes?

Start to notice the shifts that take place when you do any or all of these things. Don't take my word for any of it. See what you experience for yourself.

Self-awareness is perhaps the most important component of the End Overwhelm Now process. The best way to cultivate self-awareness is to do so in the spirit of curiosity. Be curious about what you're saying to yourself and how you're working yourself up. Be curious about what happens if you change around a few words in your head and see what shifts in your body and emotions, in your focus and your mind. This process is not about judgement or increasing pressure on yourself. To the contrary, it is about *understanding* first and foremost. It's also about developing compassion for how unconscious processes have caused you so much stress and suffering in your life. Judging and blaming are the last things I want you to start doing . . . not only because I wrote this book for the sole purpose of helping you, but also because both of those actually *increase* the overwhelm.

So, don't do that! Your assignment for right now is just to "play catch" with your patterns – make it a game to see how many you can catch in a day -- and celebrate the fact that just by increasing your awareness, you've taken the first step toward changing them.

When I first read the following poem, I was struck by the parallel with *End Overwhelm Now*. Portia Nelson's metaphor of repeatedly falling into a hole represents how we can learn to correct our habitual behaviors. You CAN choose to "walk down another street" and end your overwhelm.

"There's a Hole in My Sidewalk"
Autobiography in Five Short Chapters

Chapter One
I walk down the street.
There is a deep hole in the sidewalk.
I fall in.
I am lost . . . I am helpless.
It isn't my fault . . .
It takes forever to find a way out.

Chapter Two
I walk down the same street.
There is a deep hole in the sidewalk.
I pretend I don't see it.
I fall in again.
I can't believe I am in this same place.
But it isn't my fault.
It still takes a long time to get out.

Chapter Three
I walk down the same street.
There is a deep hole in the sidewalk.
I see it there.
I still fall . . . it's a habit . . . but,
My eyes are open.
I know where I am.
It is my fault.
I get out immediately.

Chapter Four
I walk down the same street.
There is a deep hole in the sidewalk.
I walk around it.

Chapter Five
I walk down another street.

Chapter 7

Now What?

*"If I keep on saying to myself that I cannot do a certain thing,
it is possible that I may end by really becoming incapable of
doing it. On the contrary, if I have the belief that I can do it, I
shall surely acquire the capacity to do it."*
~ Mahatma Gandhi, activist, leader

To end overwhelm, we have to change our minds. There are no time management or people management strategies that will solve your overwhelm unless you change the Beliefs, Language, Attention and Behavior that created your overwhelm in the first place. This chapter is intended to help you take what you've learned, and apply it in your life.

SHIFTING PERSPECTIVES

To implement what you've learned about overwhelm, the following shifts in perspective will be of great service to you:

Choose To Be "At-Cause"

We're used to living in a world where outside influences seek to tell us what to do. As young children, we acted in response to our parents and other family members. Once in school, teachers told us what to do. Friends, fellow students and the school culture also applied various norms of thinking and behaving. As we grew up, we faced the societal demands of college, jobs, relationships, family, material wealth, and countless other influences. It's no surprise that many of us feel "at the effect" of the world around us. My client Joanna described this as a huge wave washing over her. Because of feeling at the effect of her circumstances, rather than the active force or the "cause," she felt powerless in her own life. She didn't think she could say no to any request, couldn't ask for what she really needed, and didn't have the resources to help with the tsunami of responsibilities.

Joanna learned to take charge of herself and her over-committed schedule. She stopped living at the effect of the world around her and became the cause in her own life. The best, and possibly the *only*, realistic way to end your overwhelm is by your choice to be at-cause in your life.

What does being at-cause mean? It means taking responsibility for your experience. It means recognizing that you are more powerful and capable than you may recognize. Being at-cause means becoming a creative problem solver in resolving your overwhelm. It means you don't give responsibility for your happiness and sanity to anyone else. In his book *Success Principles*, Jack Canfield says, "Take 100% responsibility for your life." It's not always easy, which is why it's not the popular choice. Yet with some practice, you'll discover it's the most empowering, uplifting way to live your life.

Being at-cause also means recognizing yourself as the cause of your problems. That's not a bad or blaming thing. To the contrary, its great benefit is that it gives you the power to solve almost every problem in your life. You're no longer a victim. It's *empowering* to know that you are the cause and the solution of most of the problems in your life.

Those who choose to be at-cause and take responsibility for their overwhelm often discover a side benefit that's almost magical. As *you* change, those around you may also change. I am not suggesting you do things to manipulate others to change or things to change. To the contrary, I'm suggesting you focus on yourself as the change agent in your life. But what does tend to happen is that as *you* become clearer, more focused, and more intentional about your approach and behavior, relationship dynamics automatically change. My clients know that seeking to change others never works – and believe me, they've tried. However, they are often amazed that changing themselves turned out to be the catalyst for the change they wanted in a relationship. The magic seems to come from simply taking responsibility and acting with the intention of bettering themselves and the dynamics at play in their lives.

Embrace A Growth Mindset

In addition to taking full responsibility as the "cause" rather than the "effect" in your own life, another important shift in perspective as you embark on the journey of eradicating overwhelm is having a wide open mind, i.e., being open to new approaches and perspectives. The book *Mindset: The New Psychology of Success* by Carol Dweck presents two opposing mindsets. A "fixed mindset" means you believe that you are unable to change your talents and abilities. As a result, you see yourself as always being who you are now, unable to change. A "growth mindset" means you believe that you are capable of growth; you see yourself as a work in progress. Through Dweck's research as a Professor of Psychology at Stanford, she found that we have the ability to change a fixed mindset -- *and there is very clear evidence that it's worthwhile to do so. People with a growth mindset are happier and more successful than those with a fixed mindset.* According to Dweck, *when you believe that you have the ability to successfully change* (e.g., end your overwhelm) *you are already on the path to making it happen.*

The Problem Is Not The Problem

There's one more change in perspective to lay the groundwork to end overwhelm now. A business saying that helps leaders shift perspective is: "The problem is not the problem." That sounds circular, but here's what it means: What you think is your problem is often not the problem.

For example, you think your problem with overwhelm is that you have too much to do, but that is not actually the problem. Instead, it's the *symptom* of some other problem. As we've discussed, sometimes the problem is that you think you have to do it all, or you have to do it perfectly, or it all has to be done now, or that somehow other people should be different than they are. So having too much to do turns out not to be the problem, rather it is these perspectives. And when these perspectives seem to be the problem, you discover that there is a solution by choosing to shift your beliefs and LAB.

Melanie is a great example. Over the course of three years, she successfully doubled her financial services business. However, more clients and more employees meant that Melanie was more overwhelmed than ever before. As we explored the greatest source of her overwhelm, it wasn't simply the business schedule; she had grave concerns about the diminishing quality of service the company was delivering when service had always been the hallmark of her firm. Poor quality, in Melanie's view of the world, meant losing clients which, ultimately, meant "death" to her. No wonder she was overwhelmed! This was a great "reveal" but probing even more deeply into "the problem is not the problem" Melanie ultimately realized that the real problem that was eating at her was a staffing decision that she had been avoiding. She was so averse to replacing a particular employee that she was tolerating standards below her integrity level. Once she uncovered what the real problem was, named her fear and turned to face it, there was a marked shift in her demeanor. Melanie still had the exact same workload (which just an hour before she had characterized as "overwhelming"). Yet, as we finished our coaching session, Melanie's sense of overwhelm was gone. She had a sense of clarity and peace and knew exactly what she needed to do. It wasn't going to be easy to let this employee go, but she was calm and clear and grounded and resourceful . . . all of which are the opposite of overwhelm. And she got there simply by being willing to see deeply into what the "problem" actually was.

If you're willing to explore -- with an open mind, a curiosity, and a true willingness to see (rather than defend) -- *the problem is not the problem* is a wonderful exercise to undertake in relation to overwhelm. The "problem" of your overwhelm then becomes the opportunity to learn about yourself, see what's really going on, take control of your Beliefs, Language, Attention and Behavior, and start to create the life you really want.

Choose to Begin Now

I entitled this book *End Overwhelm Now* because my goal is to empower you to recognize how you create overwhelm, and give you the tools and perspective to stop it *now*, if you choose. You may have the best of intentions to create change, but turning intentions into action, and action into habits, is a more complicated process. To help you on your way, I've created the worksheet below to support you in the process of change. The worksheet is also available at www.EndOverwhelmNow.com. Please take a moment *now* to *decide* you're ready to change the pattern of overwhelm in your life and to *choose* even the smallest shifts to end your overwhelm. Get clarity on why you *must* create the change now. Then *act*: pick just a few actions to get started. You may even want to enlist the support of a friend (possibly someone who is overwhelmed too) who can help you follow through on these commitments to yourself.

For ongoing support on your *End Overwhelm Now* journey, join us on Facebook, **www.facebook.com/endoverwhelmnow** and Pinterest, **www.pinterest.com/coachkaren0217** to keep the momentum.

Personal Action Plan to End Overwhelm Now

DYNAMICS	OPTIONS	YOUR PLAN
1) If I can't keep up I'll die	Physical reactions: • Take several deep breaths • Smile • Listen to your choice of relaxing music Psychological reaction: • What are you really afraid of? • WAM-it exercise	I choose to implement the following when I feel that if I can't keep up I'll die:

Three Triggers of "Stacking and Lacking"

DYNAMICS	OPTIONS	YOUR PLAN
a. It's too much	Organize the excess: 1. Ask: "What *SPECIFICALLY* is causing me to feel overwhelmed right now?" 2. Write down your answer, generally 4 – 6 items 3. Write down 1 – 2 *small* next steps for each 4. Which of these actions would most help your feeling of overwhelm? How can you complete that one action? Who can help? 5. Acknowledge yourself for making the decision to shift the feeling.	I choose to implement the following when there's too much or I'm stacking:
b. There's not enough	• Challenge your thinking: Is it true? • Create your own list of empowering resources	I choose to implement the following when I am lacking:
c. I'm not enough	• Catch yourself in unrealistic comparisons • Make a list of your many strengths, capabilities and accomplishments • Be willing to call on your resources	I choose to implement the following when I feel I'm not enough:

LAB: Language, Attention and Behavior

DYNAMICS	OPTIONS	YOUR PLAN
Language	• Ban the bully • Avoid absolutes • Stop shoulding on yourself • Replace lousy questions with powerful ones • Eavesdrop on yourself	What language patterns do I use to create overwhelm?
Attention	• Intentionally practice paying attention • Notice how attention affects your emotions • Override defaults • Organize your thinking • Focus on what you can control	
Behavior	• Take even the smallest actions by chunking/ celebrating and planning • Start anywhere and before you're ready • Get support • Leverage the power of habit • Take care of your body	Which of my behaviors contribute to overwhelm? What behaviors will I choose now?

To conclude Section I of this book, I'd like you to meet Joyce. She is a financial professional with a busy practice, four employees, a husband and kids, and a desperate wish for peace of mind and time for herself. She was one of the first clients with whom I shared the STORIES process you'll read in the next section. Initially, she was overwhelmed much of the time. But she was committed to having a different experience of herself and her life. She followed the End Overwhelm Now program and even kept the concepts that you've learned where she could see them all the time. Back then, she kept her End Overwhelm Now instructions on Post-It notes on her desk.

She was dedicated to the practice of catching herself, and especially to asking herself what *specifically* was causing her feeling of overwhelm *in the moment* when she felt overwhelm building.

She focused on what she did best, and got better about asking for support and utilizing her resources. As her financial services business grew, she had further opportunities to manage her overwhelm, and she held the belief that she could figure it out. I spoke to her recently as she was preparing to go on a two-week European vacation (yes, finally getting that time for herself). She described how busy she was, preparing to be gone from her business for two weeks. We celebrated together as she said, "That old feeling of overwhelm started to creep in and I just said, 'No, I'm not going to do that now.' Instead, I kept focusing on what I needed to be ready for my trip." Joyce had created a new story of empowerment and focused action that carried her through even the most challenging of times.

That is my wish for you – that you will catch yourself as that old pattern begins, and to choose a more empowered response. In Section III, you'll read case stories of people who have their own busy lives and challenges. Yet they all benefited from understanding the power of their Beliefs, Language, Attention and Behavior.

One of my favorite quotes is from Thomas Edison. He said, "If we did all the things we are capable of, we would literally astound ourselves."

The next time you start to slip into your old pattern of overwhelm, catch your Beliefs, your Language, your Attention, your Behavior, then remember what you are capable of, remember that the power to choose is yours . . . and astound yourself.

Emergency Intervention

The 7-Step STORIES Process to End Overwhelm NOW

Section II

THE 7 STEP STORIES PROCESS

"You must take personal responsibility. You cannot change the circumstances, the seasons, or the wind, but you can change yourself. That is something you have charge of."
~ *Jim Rohn, author and speaker*

If you are feeling overwhelmed right now, like right this minute, the 7-step STORIES process will get you out of your overwhelmed state immediately. Give yourself the gift of spending 20 minutes to walk through it step-by-step. At the end, I promise you will feel restored to sanity.

You must actually do each step – in order – for it to work. You can't just simply read through each step or think about them; you have to actually *do them.*

If you are currently in a state of overwhelm, your tendency will be to scan through these pages looking for a silver bullet. It's a natural reaction, but it won't work to end your overwhelm now. You're going to have to follow the steps. But it won't take long, and I promise it will be well worth your time. At the end, you will surprised how calm and grounded and resourceful you will feel.

Getting Ready

You're about to embark on a quick rescue process that will engage your mind and body to *interrupt the cycle* of overwhelm. In Chapter 3 of this book, I describe the radical premise for ending overwhelm now which is this:

> Overwhelm doesn't come from the external circumstances in your life; and it isn't eliminated by magic strategies to deal with what's happening "out there." Overwhelm is the result of *internal* processes, patterns and responses – and they're within your control.

My definition of overwhelm is this: *a physical, emotional and psychological* **reaction** *to a pattern of beliefs, language, attention and behavior.*

In other words, **overwhelm is a reaction to how you are processing the outside world.**

As real as your overwhelm may feel in this moment, changing your Beliefs, Language, Attention and Behavior will break your cycle of overwhelm. What you choose to focus on, what you say to yourself, the importance you give to those thoughts in your head, and how you act (or don't act) as a result, all of these contribute to your unique cycle of overwhelm. Your mind always has a running dialogue; without conscious intervention, that dialogue becomes a story you believe. You may even have a story right now about whether this book can truly help you. Stories are a major part of your overwhelm. And now the STORIES process will be the first step on your path to freedom.

STORIES

STORIES is an acronym for the 7-step process I developed to help my clients out of their cycles of overwhelm. Follow each of the steps in order, and do the few actions associated with each.

Don't freak out; this isn't going to take all day. Each step only takes a few minutes. The action steps are in bold text so you can quickly go through the process once you understand the concepts. Just take it one simple step at a time. Doing this will move you out of overwhelm, and you'll be training your brain to think in the ways that will help to end your overwhelm forever.

The STORIES acronym stands for:

S – STOP!

T – Take a Step Back

O – Organize Your Thinking

R – Remember Your Resources

I – Identify What's Within Your Control

E – Engage a New Story

S – Schedule Next Steps

As we go through each step, I will be illustrating how it works at the bottom of each page using the example of a client. I call her Renee, though that is not her real name. At the time I took her through the STORIES process, Renee was facing finals week in her second semester of medical school. When we met, she presented me with a mind-spinning list of finals, papers due, and presentations she had to prepare for. It was all important, all urgent, and way too much for her mind to juggle. She was in that near-to-breaking overwhelm state where her mind was telling her "I cannot handle this."

But she could, and she did.

My goal is that you will, too.

Get Set

Here's how we start:

1) CHOOSE to take a few minutes right now to change your cycle of overwhelm, even if you think you don't have time. You will be so much more productive when we're done that it will more than make up for the few minutes you spend following the process.

2) DECIDE that you *can* shift out of your overwhelm and you are *going to.*

3) ACT now by starting with a piece of paper and a pen. Don't use a computer, tablet or phone; it's better to write your answers on paper.

4) IGNORE the voice in your head shouting that you don't have time for this, or that it won't work. How often is that voice actually right?

5) WRITE down all your answers either using the worksheet below, downloading the worksheet from
www.EndOverwhelmNow.com/Downloads
or using whatever paper you have on hand.

WORKSHEET FOR THE 7-STEP STORIES PROCESS to
END OVERWHELM NOW

Step	Summary	Your Notes
1) STOP	Tell yourself "STOP!" Take several deep breaths.	
2) TAKE A STEP BACK	Shift your physiology. Shift your perspective.	
3) ORGANIZE	What SPECIFICALLY is causing your feeling of overwhelm right now? Write it down and be specific. What's one next step?	
4) REMEMBER YOUR RESOURCES	What are your strengths, abilities, skills? Who can help you? What knowledge or skills are needed? Where can you find or learn that? What financial resources are needed? What activities or commitments can you delegate, delay, or dump?	

Step	Summary	Your Notes
5) IDENTIFY CONTROL AREAS	Focus on what you CAN control, and let go of what you can't.	I can control (hint: it's only you): I can't control:
6) ENGAGE A NEW STORY	What new beliefs, perspectives, language, or stories would allow you to move forward powerfully?	
7) SCHEDULE	Put your discoveries and action steps in your calendar to free your mind.	

STOP!

STOP

Changing your overwhelm starts with just a few seconds of intention.

Stop whatever you are doing.

Shift your focus for just a minute and take the time to recognize that you're in overwhelm.

Tell yourself "STOP!" Say that powerful word out loud. Say it twice if you want. Let yourself hear the command you are claiming with that one word.

Make the conscious decision to gain control. The chicken-with-its-head-cut-off franticness is not serving you, so stop.

Remember: You are strong, competent and capable of handling whatever you need to face. As overwhelming as the situation may be, YOU are more powerful and capable than you recognize right now.

Take five deep breaths: Inhale deeply for 5 seconds, hold briefly and exhale for 5 seconds. Focus on slow and controlled breathing. You can even make the sound, "Aaaaahhhhh," as you exhale. Do not rush through this part. We are literally talking about a minute for all five breaths . . . well 65 seconds to be exact.

Now congratulate yourself for taking the first step. Seriously. Take another second and acknowledge yourself for taking charge to end your overwhelm.

Application/Example for Step 1:

When Renee came to our coaching call, she felt incapacitated by all she had to do, but at the same time, she was under tremendous pressure to get everything done because of looming deadlines. Taking a moment to interrupt her worried thinking and take a few deep breaths helped Renee ground herself in the present moment (nothing was on fire, no one was dying) and put herself into a state where she could focus on the next important steps.

NOTES

TAKE A
STEP BACK

TAKE A
STEP BACK

Shift your perspective to start taking control.

Literally stand up and take a step back right now. From a different vantage point, new solutions become possible.

Ending overwhelm right now requires you to Take a Step Back in two ways:

- **You must shift your physiology, which shifts the physical reaction of overwhelm.**

  Overwhelm has a physical energy that prevents you from thinking clearly, even when you know you need to. Yet most of us are so used to "living in our heads" that we forget that to shift the mind, it can help to shift the body.

- **You must shift your perspective, which shifts the mental churn of overwhelm.**

  Overwhelm often comes from seeing the situation or problem as bigger than it actually is, while seeing yourself as smaller, or less powerful, than you really are. Reverse that perception, and you're on your way to ending your state of overwhelm.

Shift Your Physiology

This step is important even if you are not aware of a physical component to your overwhelm. If you are aware that you are caught up in a strong physical reaction, physically taking a step back is especially important in shifting the energy. In this case, take a minute to **notice specifically where in your body you're feeling the sense of overwhelm.** Direct your attention there. Bring it into your conscious awareness. Awareness is the first step in any kind of change. Notice where there is tension in your body, and be intentional about relaxing it. When your body is stiff and tense, it reinforces the mind's message that you're in a state of stress.

Unless you're in a situation where it really isn't possible, take just 30 seconds to get up and move...right now. Swing your arms, roll your shoulders, relax your face, keep breathing deeply. If you have pent-up energy that's keeping you from thinking clearly, see if you can find a way to release some of it . . . obviously only if it's appropriate. Do something even if it feels silly: stomp around, pummel a pillow, growl or release a yell. The physical tension of overwhelm is real. Recognizing and then physically releasing it helps physiologically. It also helps psychologically because moving your position in space literally shifts your perspective (*from where I'm standing* . . . .) which helps your brain with shifting *its* perspective. Sounds silly but it's true.

Shift Your Perspective

When you SEE different, you will BE different. This is not an over-simplification; it's true that when you see a situation differently, it shifts you internally, shifts your response. How you see your situation and how you feel about the situation are what is causing your overwhelm. They are also the path *out* of overwhelm.

The view is different when you take a step up, down, forward or back. A good metaphor is to imagine that you are facing a wall (or problem), standing right up against it, your nose practically touching. What do you see? Just the wall (or problem) directly in front of your face, and nothing else. Now do one of two things. Take a few steps back and notice how much more you are able to see. Or simply turn around and face the other direction. Now you see an entirely different view. Interrupting your cycle of overwhelm is like that – take a different view. Not just the six inches right in front of your face.

The goal here is to see your own situation—what you think is causing you to feel overwhelmed – in a different, more empowering way. Shifting perspective, sending your brain a new message, such as: "I'll figure this out," or "I can handle this one step at a time" can markedly change how you feel. Your mind just needs the reassurance that there's a way out. Changing your physicality in space actually helps to send your mind a different message.

Congratulate yourself for completing Step 2 of ending your overwhelm.

Application/Example for Step 2:

I asked Renee to walk around as she told me about her list of assignments due over the next few days. The movement automatically helped her feel less "frozen" by it all. We acknowledged that it WAS a lot to handle. It was natural to react to having so much to do in a short time. That small shift then helped her also recognize that she had already done a lot of the prep work. We helped her see the tasks ahead as incremental steps instead of feeling that she was "starting from scratch" with the assignments. Rather than feeling like there was an impossible barrier in front of her, Renee realized it was manageable by creating a plan.

ORGANIZE

ORGANIZE

Organize your thinking to end overwhelm.

Chapter 6 of this book explains that the brain needs to be able to recognize patterns. When an orchestra is warming up there is a cacophony of unpleasant sounds. But as soon as the orchestra comes together, as soon as a pattern is formed, the noise becomes beautiful music. Remember a time when you organized a room, a drawer, maybe some paperwork. How great did that feel?

When struggling with overwhelm, your pattern of thinking creates a jumble of thoughts, feelings and actions, which creates that "Oh my God, I will *never* be able to _____." When that happens, the part of your brain responsible for fight or flight behavior kicks in . . . and believe me, that is NOT a resourceful state. Neither flight nor fight nor freeze helps you one bit when faced with a mountain of tasks or responsibilities.

Step 3 takes just a few minutes, but it will engage your brain in a way that helps to create order from the chaos swirling around in there, which helps calm your brain and therefore calm your overwhelm.

First, take a moment to clearly identify what is most triggering your feeling of being overwhelmed:

- Are you telling yourself *it's all too much*? This comes from mentally *stacking* too many to do's, too many challenges, too many responsibilities, and giving yourself too much for your mind to track. In this case, organizing will involve prioritizing and chunking what you have to do into manageable pieces.

- **There's not enough:** If you are creating your sense of overwhelm by telling yourself that there is not enough time, not enough money, not enough knowledge, not enough resources, etc. then this step may involve listing (organizing) your resources so your brain can recognize that you actually do have what you need. This gives you a more realistic perspective and reassures you that it can be done.

- **I'm not enough:** Focusing on what you, yourself lack --lack of knowledge, training, a degree, experience, wishing you were younger or older or anything you're not, feeling lacking in comparison to others -- all disempowers you in a way that creates a state of overwhelm. In this case, organizing involves being realistic about your capabilities. Being critical or excessively demanding of yourself does not help you get out of overwhelm or accomplish anything. The next step, Remember Your Resources, will also support you in managing this trigger.

Sometimes overwhelm is driven by a combination of these forces, but usually one is the primary driver. Which is most in play for you right now?

Once you have identified what limiting beliefs and language (what you are saying to yourself) are in play, then ask yourself:

WHAT *SPECIFICALLY* IS CAUSING ME TO FEEL OVERWHELMED *RIGHT NOW?*" It can be helpful to ask this question out loud, or have someone else ask you the question.

1) **Write down, *as specifically as you can*, each answer that comes to mind.** This isn't your to-do list; these are the *few things*

that are causing you to feel overwhelmed. Most people list four to seven causes before their minds go blank for a moment. That's your list to focus on. You may be tempted to add more reasons to your list because there's so much going on in your head. But to end your cycle of overwhelm in the moment, you only have to address the few things that came up as your first answer to the question.

When I say **be specific**, I mean don't write "my job" or "leaving for vacation" or "Jack and Nancy arriving on Sunday." I mean write *exactly* what at work is weighing on you, and if it's a specific project, what about that specific project is causing you the most worry and distress? If it's leaving town, what part of it is weighing on you most heavily? What specifically about the upcoming visit feels overwhelming to you?

2) What's really **most important** about that item on the list? And what is the real outcome? We often get fixated on the tasks, and forget why we're stressing ourselves out over them. If it's not that important, or that urgent, you can intentionally take it off the "overwhelm" list.

3) Next, **think of just the next one to two small steps** you could take to resolve or move each of those items forward, even just a little. **Write those steps down** as well. You have now identified concrete steps to resolve the emotional and mental swirl of overwhelm! You have also engaged the logical, executive function part of your brain to organize your thinking.

Application/Example Step 3

Step 3 of the STORIES process was the most important step for Renee, and it only took about 10 minutes. Although Renee's perspective had opened to include the possibility of success, it still felt like too much because it was a disorganized jumble in her mind. We had to find a way to set some priorities and time frames to create a manageable plan. So we did the following:

1) We listed the upcoming requirements by day and created a simple calendar of demands. Even though it seemed like a huge list in Renee's mind, it was really just 12 specific assignments.

2) Then we prioritized the demands. If an exam had a 30% effect on her grade, and a paper was only worth 5% of her grade, we allocated more prep time to the exam. She could then relax if the paper wasn't "perfect."

3) With a clear view of the priorities, we did a quick guess of how much work was needed for the minimum preparation for each task. With the action steps, the priorities, and the due dates, we created a three-day action plan for success.

From these few steps, Renee had a clear vision for how to best use her time. Rather than overwhelm, she had peace of mind by understanding her greatest risks and preparing for them.

S T O R I E S

REMEMBER
YOUR
RESOURCES

REMEMBER YOUR RESOURCES

Your Resources Can Help You Overcome Your Overwhelm

Because overwhelm is a fear-based reaction, it makes you think in limited ways – typically fight, flight, or freeze. As you intentionally redirect your focus right now, know that you have an answer to what's causing your overwhelm (because you DO!). Any of the three triggers for overwhelm – *it's too much, there's not enough, and I'm not enough* – can be neutralized by taking just a minute or two to recognize that there *is* a solution.

Simply start a list of the resources available to you that can help you take charge of the things that seem overwhelming. Use the examples below and **take just one to two minutes to create your own list of resources**. These may include:

- Your strengths, abilities, skills. Where in your life have you successfully handled something like this, or even more stressful or complicated than this? What talents could you leverage more fully?

- People you know who can offer:

  o information you need,
  o encouragement or emotional support,
  o connections to other people or resources, or
  o time, talents or abilities you need.

Our ancestors thrived in community, but today we often feel isolated. What community members can you call on for support?

- Specific knowledge or skills needed. Where could you learn that, who could help you, or who could you hire? Get creative, and don't let the "well, that will never work" voice shut you down.

- Financial resources. If you perceive money to be an obstacle, how much do you *realistically* need, and what are a few options for financial support? Remember your community.

- Time resources. If you perceive time to be an obstacle, what activities or commitments can you delegate, delay, or dump?

If you can't come up with any resourceful ideas yourself, make an appointment to brainstorm this list with someone else who can see the situation more objectively than you can right now. There is almost always a solution to any task, problem or challenge you're facing. Your situation has been faced and overcome by someone somewhere. You may just need the support of someone else to help you find that solution.

When we're overwhelmed, we tend to isolate; to end overwhelm, it can help to collaborate. That's why it's helpful to remember that you are surrounded by resources. With internet access and the ability to communicate and reach around the world, there are unlimited resources – more resources than in the history of mankind. We must just remember that we won't see those resources unless and until we look for them.

Acknowledge Yourself for taking these steps to end your overwhelm. Seriously, take a minute and notice what you just did, that you took a constructive and supportive step.

Application/Example Step 4

Examining the resources available to Renee to support the actions she identified in Step 3 looked like this:

1) Renee began with her overwhelming list of tasks (trigger of "It's too much"). We used the resource of the instructors' priorities (weight of each assignment toward her grade) to set her priorities. Knowing where to focus her time and energy allowed Renee to set herself up to succeed.

2) To build Renee's confidence (trigger of "I'm not enough"), we looked at how to apply her strengths. She recognized that she was really good at learning, which helped her feel more in control of some of her assignments. The presentation she had to deliver was a weak area. Renee admitted that it was a big contributor to her feeling of overwhelm. Looking at her resources, she identified a fellow classmate who could coach her to do a better job.

3) Instead of focusing on the lack of time (trigger of "there's not enough"), we re-framed it as a resource to manage. With the prioritized plan created in Step 3, Renee was able to feel in control of her time again.

IDENTIFY

IDENTIFY

YOUR SCOPE OF CONTROL

Focus on what you CAN control.

There's an old saying that failing to forgive someone is like taking poison and expecting the other person to die. Similarly, when we spend our precious mental, emotional and physical energies fighting against the things we can't change, it is only we who suffer.

Look at the list of things that are overwhelming you and ask:

What is within your direct control?

What can you influence?

And what is totally outside your control?

When you are worrying about the things you can't control, all three of the overwhelm triggers are in effect. If it's outside you're control, it's too much to handle, there aren't enough resources, and you're not enough to resolve it. Of course this would lead to overwhelm!

If after doing Steps 1-4 you are still in the throes of overwhelm, we need to make sure you are focusing on the things you *can* control, or at least influence. People often focus on trying to "control" other people. This doesn't work. I haven't met anyone who wants to be controlled by another person. The best you can do is seek to *influence* another. As the illustration below shows, when we're overwhelmed we tend to focus more on what we *can't* control or influence, rather than what we can.

Looking at the list of what is causing your feelings of overwhelm, and the actions you've identified to begin to manage it, ask the following questions:

1) **What can I do about it right now?** You will feel a sense of empowerment when you can take specific action now. In Chapter 6 we talk a lot about the power of taking action. For now, just trust me that the best thing you can do is to do *something*.

2) **If I can't do anything about it right now, then when** can **I act on it?** For example, if you're reading this on Sunday morning, and you need to contact a business that's open on Monday, write down a reminder for the specific action to take on Monday, and then *let it go* until then. To continue to worry your mind, visiting and re-visiting it mentally, is a totally unproductive energy drain. It reinforces the message to your brain and your body that you are out of control when you are *not*.

3) **If I can't do anything about it right now, and I can't do anything about it later, is it really something I can control or influence? If not, how can I let it go?** Recognize that holding on to something you can't change is hurting yourself and others. If your mind just won't let it go, experiment with scheduling a date to worry about it in the future. If the worry comes up again, remind yourself you have an appointment to think about it later. When it's time for your scheduled "worry appointment," go through this series of questions again. See if there's now something you can control. If not, do you really want to spend your valuable time and energy on the topic? If you must, set another appointment in the future until you choose to really let go.

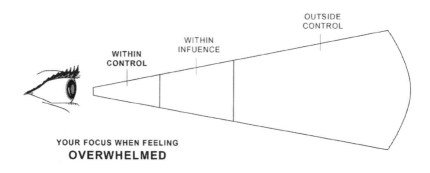

YOUR FOCUS WHEN FEELING
OVERWHELMED

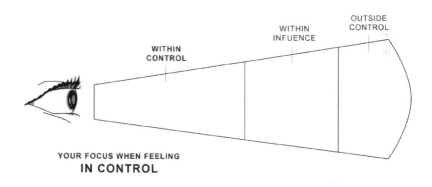

YOUR FOCUS WHEN FEELING
IN CONTROL

Application/Example Step #5

Renee admitted that she was especially nervous about a "stand and deliver" presentation for one of her classes. She worried about being stumped by the questions, giving the wrong answer, and looking foolish in front of the class. Of course, the more she focused on this, the more overwhelmed she became. She couldn't control the questions asked or the reactions of her classmates. So we focused on what she could do to best prepare, and intentionally let go of everything else.

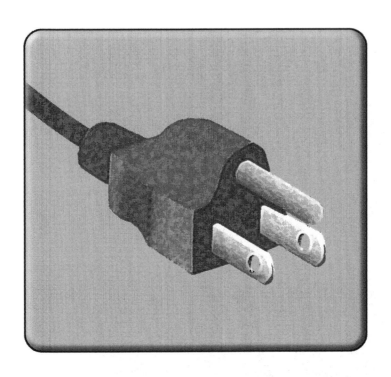

STORIES

ENGAGE AN EMPOWERING NEW STORY

ENGAGE A NEW STORY

Engage a new, more empowering story free of overwhelm.

Your old pattern of Language, Attention and Behavior is the foundation of your overwhelm. Creating new patterns is what will rescue you. Anyone who has quit an addictive habit (such as smoking or drinking) had to find alternative behaviors to replace the old. Similarly, you must have an intentional focus of what you want to move *toward* in place of your old habit of being overwhelmed, to avoid falling back into it.

So, right here and now you're going to create a new pattern of Language and Attention that's your alternative to overwhelm:

Take just a few minutes and write down your answers to each of these questions:

- *How do I prefer to be handling the challenges before me?* Would you prefer to be focused, calm, confident, happy, _____?

- **How would I prefer to feel about myself and my capabilities?** How would your overwhelm change if you considered yourself competent, capable, intelligent, wise, prepared, and powerful?

- *What would help me put this situation in perspective?* Overwhelm often arises when we fail to connect with our values and priorities in life, so *everything* seems both urgent and important – a matter of life or death. Once you identify priorities, you can reassure yourself that the situation is manageable and survivable. You might even recognize it's perfectly designed to help you grow.

- *How will my supportive resources change my story?* In the Remember Your Resources step you identified that you don't have to be alone in managing this situation. Your new story can recognize the support that's available to you.

- *What words or statements would be consistent with my new story?* What could you say to yourself that would help you think and feel the ways you described above? Jot down a few phrases.

- *What are some effective ways to remind myself to practice my new story instead of my old story of how overwhelming it all is and how overwhelmed I am?* For example, you might put a reminder in your phone, have a picture on your desk, or play a certain song in your car.

Recognize that your ability to shift from your cycle of overwhelm to intentional focus, emotions and actions gives you control and freedom in your life.

Application/Example Step #6

Renee engaged a new story that staying focused and following her plan guaranteed success. She took pride in being able to juggle such an impressive list of demands; even staying calm and engaged through it all. She set up reminders on her phone to take just a moment to imagine herself being successful in her final assignments. This helped keep her attention on success, rather than fear. Any time she caught herself slipping into her old story of overwhelm, she brought her attention back to the new story.

STORIES

SCHEDULE
NEXT STEPS

SCHEDULE NEXT STEPS

Schedule your important steps to end overwhelm.

This last step involves taking focused action.

Action matters, no matter how small.

Procrastination and distraction are the hallmarks of overwhelm, so this is the opportunity to begin training your mind to focus and take the desired action. You've identified what specifically is causing your feeling of overwhelm, you've identified a few steps to get momentum and recognized some resources to help you along the way. You've made the decision to let go of the things you can't control and to direct your attention toward what you can control or influence. You've even come up with a new pattern of language and attention to engage a new story. The last part of the pattern of LAB, described in Section I, is Behavior. You *must* take action to break your cycle of overwhelm.

Look at your notes from the exercises above and choose two or three small steps you can take now, and also schedule a few specific actions on your calendar for the future.

Commit to taking those small action steps, no matter what.

Recognize that every time you make a decision and follow through on it, no matter how small, you are training yourself to be in control of your Language, Attention and Behavior. You are training yourself to be in control of your overwhelm.

Celebrate your success in choosing decisive, focused action instead of overwhelm.

Application/Example Step #7

In about 20 minutes, Renee had a step-by-step plan for each of the three days of final projects. She knew which tasks were most important to be successful, and the times she would focus on each. Instead of focusing on EVERYTHING at once, she focused on each activity in her plan, knowing its value toward her ultimate goal. At the end of three days of intense demands, Renee celebrated a very successful semester and A's on her final projects.

S.T.O.R.I.E.S is a Process

You did it!

You DID the steps, right?

You didn't just read through them and hope for a shift.

Because this process will work for you when you make the decision to shift out of your overwhelm by taking action, including DOING the 7 steps.

If you've actually done the STORIES process, what are you noticing? Is your mind more focused? Is your body feeling any different? Where did you notice resistance to the process? I have a saying: "Resistance is the voice of future regret." If you noticed resistance, I encourage you to take a few moments to explore that. What are you afraid of? What do you have to lose by letting go of your overwhelm?

Be kind with yourself working through these questions and through this process.

If you found it hard to navigate the steps of the process alone, that's okay. Perhaps you could benefit from having someone – a friend, colleague or coach – walk you through the process. When I'm working with clients in overwhelm, I have the benefit of being independent of the situation. I have a fresh perspective to ask needed questions or notice what's working and what isn't. We all benefit from that type of independent thinking to help us see the situation more clearly. So if you were challenged by the STORIES process, consider who can help you work through it with more clarity.

If the process worked for you, great! You now have a new skill set to break your cycle of overwhelm when it sneaks up on you in the future. Over time, seek to catch yourself earlier and earlier in the cycle so you interrupt overwhelm before it takes hold.

Most important, however, is that you also read Section I. If you came straight here to the STORIES process, perfect. Now it's important to start at the beginning. That's where, instead of crisis intervention, you actually learn how to change your habitual pattern of getting into overwhelm in the first place.

Although it's great to have a life-saving intervention in case of a heart attack, wouldn't you rather eat healthy and exercise regularly to prevent the heart attack to begin with?

Section II is CPR. I hope you're breathing and your heart is pumping again. But Section I teaches you how to have an *ongoing* healthy response to the responsibilities and demands of your life. If you haven't read Section I, please do so that you can truly end your overwhelm.

This is your life. You can choose to be at the effect of -- victim to -- your habitual patters of Language, Attention and Behavior or to take charge and change your overwhelm.

Overwhelm never serves; indeed, what it does is diminish and demoralize. The world truly needs the very best version of you that you can bring. You deserve to live from your strengths, not from weakness. And your family, friends and colleagues will also benefit from your ability to break your cycle of overwhelm.

In the 1600s, Welsh poet George Herbert offered these wise words: "Do not wait; the time will never be 'just right.' Start where you stand, and work with whatever tools you may have at your command . . . ."

My great wish is that this book offers the tools and perspectives you need right now in your life to end your pattern of overwhelm and engage in your life in a resourceful, empowered and deeply satisfying way.

SECTION III

Case STORIES

In this section I present just a few of the
clients who have used the strategies in this
book to end their sense of being overwhelmed.
You will see that their overwhelm shifts by
shifting themselves – their patterns of LAB
and their beliefs - rather than by changing
the outside world. I share their stories in the
hope that you will see that no matter your
situation, you, too, can end your overwhelm
now. The tools that supported each client
in their shift are in bold text. You can find
interviews and more stories on our website:
www.EndOverwhelmNow.com

Case Stories

ANNA

Anna is a single mom juggling a more-than-full-time job, two kids, a dog and a gerbil. She's a senior project manager in a financial services technology firm. It's a job she enjoys, but it often requires more than 40 hours per week. Her 11-year-old son plays baseball, basketball and the tuba, all of which require transportation arrangements, equipment, supplies, and Anna's attention. Her 13-year-old, when not snap-chatting with friends, is a Girl Scout and budding dancer. Although the kids are supposed to be responsible for the dog and the gerbil, overseeing their care usually falls to Anna. On top of her job, the kids, the pets and running the household, at the three-year mark from her divorce, Anna would like to start dating . . . but where she would squeeze in the time for that, she doesn't know. Regular exercise, which she knows is important, well, that's just going to have to wait.

Anna knows that getting to bed at a reasonable hour is one of the most supportive things she can do for herself, but it almost never happens. She often stays up late cleaning the kitchen, doing laundry, paying her bills and her mother's bills, answering emails, making the kids lunches for the next day, etc. Her life often feels like a treadmill.

On our coaching call, Anna tells me, "There's always too much to do and I just can't keep up. No matter how fast I go and how little sleep I get, there's always more I should be doing." She says that she feels exhausted and inadequate most of the time, and often wonders, "Is this it? Is this all there is to my life?"

Her daily life is a challenge, but the unexpected things that crop up overwhelm her most of all: a meeting at school that her son forgot to mention, her boss assigning a new rush project, unexpected medical results that require additional testing. She says that these surprises feel like a physical blow to her stomach. She starts to beat herself up that she should have somehow known or anticipated these events, and doesn't see how she can now possibly fit *this* – whatever the "this" is -- into her life as well.

To stop her overwhelm cycle, we first had to interrupt her reactionary pattern when the unexpected happened. When those unexpected, but seemingly inevitable, surprises arose, Anna jumped into the STORIES process. She recognized that punch-in-the-stomach feeling as one of the starting symptoms. She learned that a *few deep breaths* would help to relax that knot. Then, using the simple process of *taking a step back* to get perspective, Anna was able to avoided descending further into overwhelm. She learned to say to herself, "Here's one of those surprises again, but I can handle it." She anticipated her default reaction of "*I'm not enough*." Instead of beating herself up and seeing herself as "inadequate," she practiced seeing herself as resilient and capable (which was also part of *engaging a new story* for her).

She learned to next *organize* what seemed to be the chaos. Anna used her project management skills (the *resource* of her *strengths*) to create a system to better manage her appointments and tasks. This step gave her clarity about her most important obligations for each day. Taking the time to identify how important each task was, how urgent, how much time it would take, or who needed to be involved, reassured her. She also reminded herself that she didn't always have to do it *now*, and she didn't always have to do it *herself*.

Anna also realized that her **patterns of language and attention** were feeding her overwhelm (feeling that her *entire schedule* was upset and catastrophizing to a worst-case scenario). Instead, when a surprise occurred, she focused on what *actually* was being disrupted, then started thinking about the **resources** she would need to take care of it. Each time Anna interrupted her cycle of overwhelm she **celebrated** with a happy-dance; this seems silly, I know, but it was effective for her, maybe just because it *was* silly and a nice shift from her usual state. She learned to take the time to **acknowledge** how she had been successful at handling the surprise. That felt much better than beating herself up and left her in an empowered and resourceful state.

The biggest surprise to Anna was how different her life was when she could keep herself from going into overwhelm. She actually *did* start anticipating the surprises better because she wasn't in that state of panic. She started prioritizing herself (instead of beating herself up). Part of that was **remembering her resources**: she found a wonderful new home for the gerbil; she worked out a reward system for the kids to care for the dog and do small household tasks instead of doing those things herself; and she found a gym near her work where she could conveniently weave stress-relieving exercise into her days.

It didn't happen overnight, but with persistence and patience, Anna continued to shift how she approached her life. She sent me an email about six months later. Not only was her relationship with her kids more relaxed and playful, but she also told me about Daniel, the new guy she was dating. By feeling better about herself and creating some space in her life, she was enjoying life so much more. "I never would have believed that simply changing how I was thinking about things would make such a huge difference," she wrote. "I don't worry about surprises anymore because I feel confident that I can handle whatever comes up now."

Case Stories

PAMELA

Pamela runs a dance school with her husband and works as a personal coach. She came to our first coaching call more than 24 hours into an overwhelm episode. She explained that she often felt so overwhelmed that it would knock her off her normal routine for a few days. Although she was used to having a lot on her plate (running a dance school, working as a coach, recently moved into a new home), she would often run into "tipping points" that knocked her off her ability to handle things. Her current tipping point was feeling behind in an advanced coach training program. She was feeling frustrated with herself because intellectually she knew she could handle it all, but the emotional reactions of panic and shame were overwhelming for her. When she felt like she just couldn't handle things, Pamela turned to the all-too-common avoidance behaviors of watching too much TV and overeating. Unfortunately these behaviors actually accelerated the feeling of overwhelm.

I explained to Pamela that we have an instinctually wired need to keep up with our environments and if we don't, we feel we might die. "That's exactly how I feel," she exclaimed, "like I'm going to die!" Although Pamela is a very competent, intelligent person, something as simple as not keeping up with the homework for her training program triggered this powerful life-or-death feeling.

As we explored Pamela's pattern of overwhelm we made several discoveries. She realized that she not only took on a lot to do, but she felt she had to do it *perfectly* (**using absolute language**). Anything less than perfection made her feel ashamed, like she had failed. She also told herself "***I'm not organized enough***" to keep up with her many projects. When her **attention** was on her perceived inability to get it all done perfectly, she felt overwhelmed. To make matters worse, Pamela also feared seeming vulnerable to others by letting them know she was overwhelmed. So she isolated herself even more by escaping into distracted behaviors. The cycle often continued for days because her behaviors perpetuated the feeling of not enough, ultimately resulting in more isolation and distracted behavior. Pamela's pattern of LAB had her firmly trapped in overwhelm.

Simply recognizing how she created the mental and emotional swirl of her overwhelm helped Pamela break her cycle. *Nothing changed in the external world*, yet Pamela felt totally different. This is often the case. Awareness of how overwhelm is created, of the erroneous beliefs we are holding, of the things we are saying to ourselves, or what we are doing in response – sometimes just making these conscious to ourselves shifts our responses.

Recognizing that her fear of not keeping up was an ancient survival mechanism, noticing it and naming it as such, immediately dissipated a lot of the "charge." She paid attention to the sensations building in her body, and learned to recognize when she needed to relax, stop, and use the tool of ***taking deep breaths*** to counteract rising tension. She learned to watch for – and catch the associated language and emotion -- when she felt ashamed of herself. That awareness allowed her to consciously choose to ***engage a new story***. Instead of shame (she ***banned her inner bully***), her story became one of empowerment by recognizing all the things that she WAS doing well. She also learned to catch when her trigger of needing to do things perfectly and feeling ashamed when she couldn't be perfect, arose (*attention affects emotions*). Instead, Pamela focused on "progress." That word (*language*) helped her feel empowered, and she could break her action steps into **small chunks** as an intentional way to achieve what she wanted.

In a recent conversation, Pamela celebrated progress on her coach training program. I teasingly asked if she still feels like she's going to die when she can't be perfect. She laughed at the very thoughts that overwhelmed her at the start. She explained that she now has the *habit* of *eavesdropping* on her conversations with herself. By simply watching out for the beliefs of *I could die* and *I'm not enough*, she can stop her overwhelm before it even begins.

Case Stories

Marcus

Marcus was laid off from his job as a newspaper reporter 10 months before our first coaching call. He had started his job search enthusiastically, but as the months went on, he felt more irrelevant and ill-prepared for the changing dynamics of his industry. The newspaper business was continually contracting as more people read their news online. Technology was also changing the reporting side of the business and things were different from how Marcus had always done them. To his credit, Marcus pursued all the right avenues for jobs: scouring online job boards and resources, reconnecting with past colleagues, going to lots of networking events, but nothing was working. As the months wore on with no new job in sight, fewer and fewer leads, and the bills piling up, Marcus felt like he was staring at a big "Dead End" sign. Any action at all felt overwhelming because he had created such a disempowering pattern of beliefs and LAB. The more time he spent around other unemployed people, the worse he felt, since the sense of overwhelm is often contagious.

Marcus was in a tough situation, no doubt about it. But the language he was using about the situation was completely disheartening and disempowering. When I had him say out loud what he was saying to himself, he was honest and told me that his internal dialog sounded like this: "There are no jobs in newspapers. And even if there were, nobody will ever hire me – I'm too old and I don't have the relevant skills." He focused and ruminated on all the negatives and on everything that *wasn't* working. As his language and attention spiraled downward, he was less inclined to take action. And even when he was able to meet with someone or got a lead, he assumed it would be another dead-end; as a result, he didn't demonstrate the skills, energy and passion that would make someone want to hire him or connect him to someone who would. The skill and passion he had demonstrated as a successful reporter was no longer visible.

Teaching Marcus to **eavesdrop** on himself so he could catch the self-defeating language was fun because the reporter in him enjoyed the technique. Although as a writer, he was a master with language, he found he needed a serious upgrade when it came to talking to himself. He had never noticed the **use of absolutes** in his self-talk, such as "*nobody* will *ever* hire me. I don't have *any* relevant skills." When Marcus heard himself say these overly dramatic – and negative -- statements out loud, he actually laughed at himself. He was determined to **write a new story** – a story of success – and shifted his language to use words like *opportunities*, *progress*, and *choosing* a new destiny.

Although the language adjustment was critical to shift Marcus's overwhelm, we also needed to change his **attention** -- what he was focusing on -- which was what he was missing. When he made a list of his strengths and accomplishments, he recognized that many of the skills and qualities he demonstrated as a reporter were a) still completely relevant despite the changes in the industry and b) quite transferrable to other industries. He discovered that his ability to ask questions, distill information, and communicate clearly are the qualities that make effective salesmen (the *resource of strengths*). Exploring this line of thinking, Marcus realized that it wasn't so much the writing that he loved in being a reporter; it was talking to people, learning their stories, and communicating ideas. We took the approach of **start anywhere and start before you're ready**. We traded Marcus' **lousy question** of, "How will I ever get a job?" to "What would I love to do?" Marcus reached out to some of his connections who had similar skills but were in different industries (**resources**). This time, though, he wasn't looking for a job. He was looking for what they loved about their careers, how they got started, and where they could see him succeeding in a similar career.

With his new focus, optimism, enthusiasm, and openness to possibly starting a new career, Marcus readily changed other **behaviors**. He focused on **what he could control**, which was upgrading his skill set. He **chunked those activities** into small, discrete steps that he then **celebrated** as an accomplishment. It had been a long since Marcus felt a sense of accomplishment. Once he felt it again, he wanted more. With this retooling of skills and renewed confidence in himself, Marcus transitioned to a sales career in the telecommunications industry. He traded the incessant deadlines of reporting for lucrative commissions.

The last time I spoke to him, Marcus was enjoying his new career immensely. Rather than a dead-end, he saw opportunity and advancement. Because he could relate so fully to others who were still struggling in their careers, Marcus had volunteered to speak to some local job search groups. He wanted to inspire others to believe in themselves and find the answer for their new career. He explained, "I thought finding a new job was about what I needed to DO. I never realized it was all about my beliefs and my thinking. I want to make sure other people know this too."

Case Stories

SAMANTHA

Samantha was an interior designer who was generally well organized. She kept most of her to-do list on a spreadsheet, which made it very easy to see what needed to be addressed. Despite her organized approach to life, she came to one of our calls incapacitated by overwhelm.

We quickly moved to the *Organize* step of the STORIES process. When asked the question, "*What specifically is causing the feeling of overwhelm right now*," Samantha replied with five answers which we wrote down. The first four were specific, manageable tasks. The fifth item on the list was, "Learn everything there is to know about" followed by an extremely complex computer program she needed for work. No wonder Samantha was overwhelmed! People spend *years* learning all the nuances of this program, and Samantha was trying to squeeze it in between taking care of the hundreds of details required by her busy practice and demanding clients.

That one task, with an unrealistic expectation that she "learn everything," triggered the "*it's too much*" feeling. It was enough to put Samantha into "freeze" mode.

So what we did was break down the single item that was her tipping point into overwhelm. We started by identifying several

resources to manage the task so that it didn't feel like it was all too much. First, she reminded herself that she didn't have to learn the program *today*, or even this week, and that learning *everything* about it was unrealistic. Next, she acknowledged out loud that she had a clear plan for learning the new program, and that she was already registered for a class that would further help her. Much of Samantha's sense of overwhelm was resolved simply by recognizing the pressure she was putting on herself, clarifying if any of the pressure was real (**is this true?**), making a plan and identifying the resources to support her.

Using just a few steps of the STORIES process took about 15 minutes, and ended the hours of overwhelm Samantha had experienced. Once we had interrupted her pattern of overwhelm, Samantha was able to remember a classic Confucius quote that she sometimes shared with her design clients: "Life is really simple, but we insist on making it complicated."

Case Stories

WILLIAM

William is a corporate trainer in a high-tech company. I was impressed with how confident he was in designing and delivering any kind of training his company needed. The prospect of teaching communication skills to a room full of senior engineers made William's eyes light up. That confidence quickly turned to overwhelm as William described the business he wanted to start. He was clear on the products and services to offer, but all the business details of creating an online training company made him panic. "I'm like the deer in the headlights," he admitted one day. "I know I *have* to move or die, but I just can't get myself to go." No matter how much good advice his friends offered, William was immoveable. In fact, the good advice just overwhelmed him with *even more* things to do.

I began by explaining the "freeze" reaction of the brain when it thinks it's under threat, and asked William to trust that we could find an answer to his challenge. I asked "***What specifically is causing your feeling of overwhelm right now about your new business?***" We had to narrow his **attention** to get to the heart of what was going on. William identified that there were two areas of the new business where he felt totally inept: the website and social media. I asked him to identify the next 1 – 2 steps that he could take in each of those areas.

That step helped us clarify that he needed some specific **resources** to help him in those areas: a web developer and a social media expert. But the prospect of hiring those resources was daunting because it was new. So we then identified some business associates who could offer recommendations.

The next worry that came up was time. William said, "I should get this all done by the end of the month." The *language* of "*should*" was starting to trigger his overwhelm again. To redirect the disempowering language, I asked about William's process for putting together a training program. He described how he put sections of the training on the floor, and physically "walked" himself through his training. Focusing on using his **strengths** reignited William's confidence. So that's how we scheduled his business activities: he put the individual steps on pieces of paper, laid them out on the floor, and "walked" himself through the steps of getting help for his business. With that, it was easy for William to **schedule** each of the activities in his calendar. Each time one of those tasks appeared on his calendar, he got excited that he was moving one step closer to his business. Instead of being frozen by the lack of clarity, he was focused on using his strengths to move forward. He even came to think of himself as a "business man" instead of a "trainer." The last I heard from William, he enjoyed the process so much he had laid out a fitness program in exactly the same way.

Case Stories

Monica

Monica is a financial planner, rapidly expanding her business. She felt like she was barely keeping up. Over a three year period, she bought two new businesses, both of which had to be integrated into her existing business. The process of acquiring additional companies created staffing, financial, client, and system integration challenges. With each acquisition, Monica grappled with overwhelm, but she had learned many helpful processes to shift or circumvent that trajectory. She was an early adopter of the STORIES process presented in this book.

On our most recent coaching call, she told me a wonderful story. She said, "I was going on vacation and had a million things to do to get ready: packing, holding the mail, boarding the dog, making sure clients were covered, getting the sprinkler fixed before I went, etc. etc. etc. I noticed the feeling of overwhelm start to come up, and I simply made a decision. I said, '*No. I choose not to be overwhelmed. I don't want to do that right now. It's not going to help anything and it's really not necessary.*' "

"*And you know what?*" she asked me. "*It worked! I didn't go into that old state of overwhelm. I stayed calm and resourceful, I focused and got done what I needed to get done, and I left for vacation pretty calm and relaxed. And then I didn't have to spend the first day of my vacation decompressing!"*

She was excited to tell me that by practicing the STORIES process and learning to shift her beliefs and her LAB patterns, she could recognize when she was headed toward overwhelm. She now feels it coming on, understands it's a mindset, and makes the decision not to go there.

She does the other things she's learned instead.

The things I taught you in this book. And she found out they work. Put into practice they actually work.

And they will work for you, too.

Case Stories

A Tale of Two Cities

This really isn't a tale of two cities – though the women do live in two different cities. It's the tale of two lives – very similar in the external details – but radically different in each woman's reaction. It is one of the best illustrations I have for demonstrating that overwhelm truly doesn't come from "out there" but is an internal reaction to the externals. As you read this comparison, see how many beliefs and patterns of langua ge, attention and behavior you notice that create the difference between these two busy women. Which patterns do you relate to?

Jessie is a single working mother of two girls. She is a lawyer at a global company, manages a team of lawyers, and does some of her own contract work. She often speaks at her alma mater to encourage young law students. Her kids are active in social and school activities. Jess has recently started a long-distance romance so visits have to be carefully coordinated to arrange for the travel. And she just – who knows why? – adopted two puppies. Even with that formidable list of things on her plate, Jessie oozes energy and enthusiasm. She sees her life as a game that she is uniquely qualified to play, and loves seeing how much she can pack into a day. Recognizing the need to recharge, she always takes time to exercise and get adequate sleep. She has very intentionally decided what to delegate (some of the child care) and what to keep (baking cupcakes for the teachers with her daughter).

Betsey provides a powerful contrast to Jess. Betsey is a married, working mother of two girls in their late teens. She is frustrated that her husband isn't more supportive of her and the children. She spends a lot of mental energy wishing her husband were different. Betsey is a junior researcher at a consulting firm. Although she is very smart and capable, Betsey doubts herself. She incessantly worries that she is just one mistake away from being fired. Although her manager reassures Betsey that he is happy with her work, she can't be convinced. She compares herself to her colleagues who have more experience, and feels she doesn't measure up, which then reinforces the cycle of self-doubt. With the anxiety around her job, Betsey tells herself she couldn't possibly take time out to exercise. The stress and overwhelm has begun to result in errors at work, and the cycle continues.

Jessie has a life that would overwhelm most of us, yet feels totally alive and fulfilled. Even with a dramatically simpler life, Betsey is overwhelmed and disempowered by her life – she feels that she is the victim of her life circumstances. If you relate more to Betsey than you do to Jessie, take heart! The tools and strategies in this book will help you create the shifts that you seek.

About the Author

Karen Van Cleve is on a mission to eradicate overwhelm. She believes that empowering thoughts and actions provide clarity and a path to achieve this goal. Karen discovered this through her own journey of discovery.

Karen began college majoring in psychology. She quickly changed her major to accounting to be able to find a job during the recession years of her early career. She worked as an accountant in the banking and property management industries. After earning her MBA, Karen discovered an enjoyment of the complexity and energy of the burgeoning technology industry. She worked for 15 years developing complex business systems for mobile telephony providers around the world. This position created the perfect laboratory for overwhelm. The impossible demands, fast pace, and unrelenting travel required her to find a way to manage her overwhelm to survive. Facing this mountain of requirements was the catalyst for change, and confronting these issues head on was a means to discovering her power and determination, re-igniting a passion for the psychology behind obtaining those tools. It wasn't until she discovered the field of coaching that she committed full-time to the practice of aiding others in beating overwhelm. She finds solidarity and inspiration in her clients, driving her to constantly learn and improve.

Karen has been blessed to work with multiple leaders in the coaching industry. She has coached clients from more than 15 countries on a variety of life and business topics. She is constantly awed by the power of the human spirit, and the infinite potential that lies within each of us.

In her continuous quest to find the fastest way to help a client achieve their peak performance, Karen has studied a variety of tools and strategies. She draws from this vast wealth of knowledge, as well as her experience with thousands of clients, to fuel her coaching, writing and speaking. As a demonstration to Karen's commitment to the synergy of community and emboldening the human experience, a portion of the proceeds of all of her books are donated to a different named charity annually. Be part of the community at www.EndOverwhelmNow.com.

47013745R00122

Made in the USA
San Bernardino, CA
21 March 2017